Microsoft A
explained

Books Available

By both authors:

BP341 MS-DOS explained
BP346 Programming in Visual Basic for Windows
BP388 Why not personalise your PC
BP400 Windows 95 explained
BP406 MS Word 95 explained
BP407 Excel 95 explained
BP408 Access 95 one step at a time
BP409 MS Office 95 one step at a time
BP420 E-mail on the Internet*
BP426 MS-Office 97 explained
BP428 MS-Word 97 explained
BP429 MS-Excel 97 explained
BP430 MS-Access 97 one step at a time
BP433 Your own Web site on the Internet
BP448 Lotus SmartSuite 97 explained
BP456 Windows 98 explained*
BP460 Using Microsoft Explorer 4 on the Internet*
BP464 E-mail and news with Outlook Express*
BP465 Lotus SmartSuite Millennium explained
BP471 Microsoft Office 2000 explained
BP472 Microsoft Word 2000 explained
BP473 Microsoft Excel 2000 explained
BP474 Microsoft Access 2000 explained
BP478 Microsoft Works 2000 explained
BP486 Using Linux the easy way*
BP488 Internet Explorer 5 explained*
BP487 Quicken 2000 UK explained*
BP491 Windows 2000 explained*
BP493 Windows Me explained*
BP498 Using Visual Basic
BP505 Microsoft Works Suite 2001 explained
BP509 Microsoft Office XP explained
BP510 Microsoft Word 2002 explained
BP511 Microsoft Excel 2002 explained
BP512 Microsoft Access 2002 explained

By Noel Kantaris:

BP258 Learning to Program in C
BP259 A Concise Introduction to UNIX*
BP284 Programming in QuickBASIC
BP325 A Concise User's Guide to Windows 3.1

Microsoft Access 2002 explained

by

P.R.M. Oliver
and
N. Kantaris

Bernard Babani (publishing) Ltd
The Grampians
Shepherds Bush Road
London W6 7NF
England

www.babanibooks.com

Please Note

Although every care has been taken with the production of this book to ensure that any projects, designs, modifications and/or programs, etc., contained herewith, operate in a correct and safe manner and also that any components specified are normally available in Great Britain, the Publishers and Author(s) do not accept responsibility in any way for the failure (including fault in design) of any project, design, modification or program to work correctly or to cause damage to any equipment that it may be connected to or used in conjunction with, or in respect of any other damage or injury that may be so caused, nor do the Publishers accept responsibility in any way for the failure to obtain specified components.

Notice is also given that if equipment that is still under warranty is modified in any way or used or connected with home-built equipment then that warranty may be void.

First Published - October 2001

British Library Cataloguing in Publication Data:

A catalogue record for this book is available from the British Library

ISBN 0 85934 512 2

Cover Design by Gregor Arthur
Printed and Bound in Great Britain by Cox & Wyman Ltd, Reading

About this Book

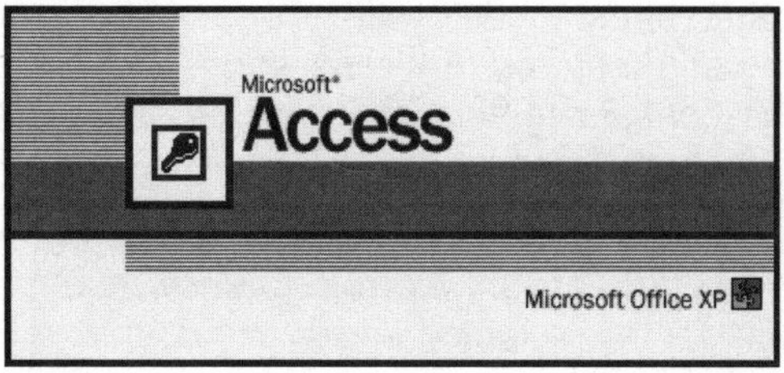

Microsoft Access 2002 explained has been written to help users to store and retrieve information using this latest Windows database from Microsoft, which is part of the Office XP suite. No previous knowledge of database design is assumed.

The book does not describe how to install Microsoft Windows, or how to set up your computer's hardware. If you need to know more about these topics, then may we suggest that you select an appropriate book from the 'Books Available' list. They are all published by BERNARD BABANI (publishing) Ltd.

In the first chapter, we give a very brief overview on database systems and we define the elements that make up an Access relational database management system. The hardware and software requirements of your system are also discussed, so that you know in advance the minimum system configuration for the successful installation and use of the package.

The next two chapters describe the working environment of the Access package, much of which is provided across the whole Office XP range of applications.

The rest of the book covers in more detail how to design and create your databases and use them to organise and structure your data using the various components of the Access system. The final chapter introduces how Access can be used with the Internet.

The major features of the package (both old and new) are discussed using simple examples that the user is encouraged to type in, save, and modify as more advanced features are introduced. This provides the new user with an example that aims to help with the learning of the most commonly used features of the package, and should help to provide the confidence needed to tackle some of the more advanced features later.

This book was written with the busy person in mind. It is not necessary to learn all there is to know about a subject, when reading a few selected pages can usually do the same thing quite adequately!

Using this book, it is hoped that you will be able to come to terms with Microsoft Access 2002 and get the most out of your computer in terms of efficiency, productivity and enjoyment, and that you will be able to do it in the shortest, most effective and informative way.

If you would like to purchase a Companion Disc for any of the listed books by the same author(s), apart from the ones marked with an asterisk, containing the file/program listings which appear in them, then fill in the form at the back of the book and send it to Phil Oliver at the stipulated address.

About the Authors

Phil Oliver graduated in Mining Engineering at Camborne School of Mines in 1967 and since then has specialised in most aspects of surface mining technology, with a particular emphasis on computer related techniques. He has worked in Guyana, Canada, several Middle Eastern countries, South Africa and the United Kingdom, on such diverse projects as: the planning and management of bauxite, iron, gold and coal mines; rock excavation contracting in the UK; international mining equipment sales and international mine consulting for a major mining house in South Africa. In 1988 he took up a lecturing position at Camborne School of Mines (part of Exeter University) in Surface Mining and Management. He retired from full-time lecturing in 1998, to spend more time writing, consulting and developing Web sites for clients.

Noel Kantaris graduated in Electrical Engineering at Bristol University and after spending three years in the Electronics Industry in London, took up a Tutorship in Physics at the University of Queensland. Research interests in Ionospheric Physics, led to the degrees of M.E. in Electronics and Ph.D. in Physics. On return to the UK, he took up a Post-Doctoral Research Fellowship in Radio Physics at the University of Leicester, and then in 1973 a lecturing position in Engineering at the Camborne School of Mines, Cornwall, (part of Exeter University), where between 1978 and 1997 he was also the CSM Computing Manager. At present he is IT Director of FFC Ltd.

Acknowledgements

We would like to thank the staff of Microsoft Press Centre for providing the software programs on which this work was based.

Trademarks

Arial and **Times New Roman** are registered trademarks of The Monotype Corporation plc.

EPSON is a registered trademark of Seiko Epson Corporation.

HP and LaserJet are registered trademarks of Hewlett Packard Corporation.

IBM is a registered trademark of International Business Machines, Inc.

Intel is a registered trademark of Intel Corporation.

Microsoft, **MS-DOS**, **Office XP**, **Windows**, **Windows NT**, **Windows Me** and **Visual Basic**, are either registered trademarks or trademarks of Microsoft Corporation.

PostScript is a registered trademark of Adobe Systems Incorporated.

TrueType is a registered trademark of Apple Corporation.

All other brand and product names used in the book are recognised as trademarks, or registered trademarks, of their respective companies.

Contents

1

Package Overview

Microsoft Access is a database management system (DBMS) designed to allow users to store, manipulate and retrieve information easily and quickly. A database is a collection of data that exists and is organised around a specific theme or requirement. It can be of the 'flat-file' type, or it can have relational capabilities, as in the case of Access, which is known as a relational database management system (RDBMS).

The main difference between flat-file and relational database systems is that the latter can store and manipulate data in multiple 'tables', while the former systems can only manipulate a single table at any given time. To make accessing the data easier, each row (or record) of data within a database table is structured in the same fashion, i.e., each record will have the same number of columns (or fields).

We define a database and its various elements as:

Database	A collection of data organised for a specific theme in one or more tables.
Table	A two-dimensional structure in which data is stored, like in a spreadsheet.
Record	A row of information in a table relating to a single entry and comprising one or more fields.
Field	A single column of information of the same type, such as people's names.

In Access 2002 the maximum size of a database is 2 gigabytes and can include linked tables in other files. The number of objects in a database is limited to 32,768, while the maximum number of fields in a table is limited to 255.

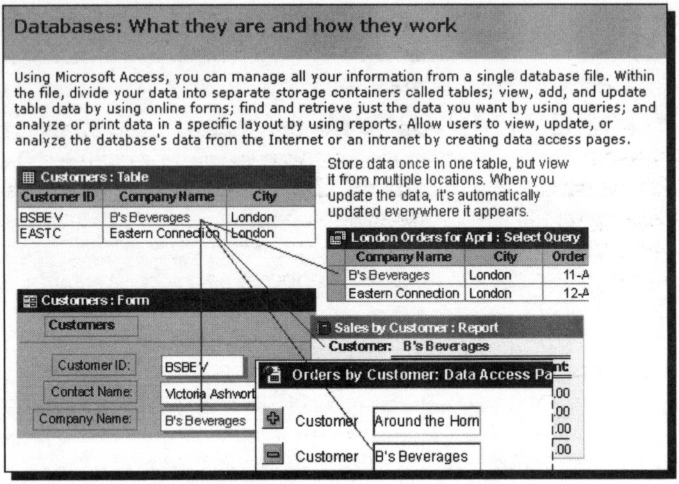

Fig. 1.1 A Graphic Introduction to Access

A good example of a flat-file database would be the invoicing details kept on its clients by a company. These details could include name of client, description of work done, invoice number, and amount charged, something like the following:

NAME	Consultancy	Invoice	Value
VORTEX Co. Ltd	Wind Tunnel Tests	9701	120.84
AVON Construction	Adhesive Tests	9702	103.52
BARROWS Associates	Tunnel Design Tests	9703	99.32
STONEAGE Ltd	Carbon Dating Tests	9704	55.98
PARKWAY Gravel	Material Size Tests	9705	180.22
WESTWOOD Ltd	Load Bearing Tests	9706	68.52

Fig. 1.2 A Flat-file Database, or Table

Such a flat-file DBMS is too limited for the type of information normally held by most companies. If the same client asks for work to be carried out regularly, then the details for that client (which could include address, telephone and fax numbers, contact name, date of invoice, etc.), will have to be entered several times. This can lead to errors, but above all to redundant information being kept on a client, as each entry would have to have the name of the client, their address, telephone and fax numbers.

The relational facilities offered by Access, overcome the problems of entry errors and duplication of information. The ability to handle multiple tables at any one time allows for the grouping of data into sensible subsets. For example, one table, called client, could hold the names of the clients, their addresses, telephone and fax numbers, while another table, called invoice, could hold information on the work done, invoice number, date of issue, and amount charged. The two tables must, however, have one unique common field, such as a client reference number. The advantage is that details of each client are entered and stored only once, thus reducing the time and effort wasted on entering duplicate information, and also reducing the space required for data storage.

Hardware and Software Requirements

If Microsoft Access 2002 is already installed on your computer, you can safely skip this and the following section of this chapter.

To install and use Access 2002, which comes as part of Professional version of Microsoft Office XP, you need an IBM-compatible PC. Microsoft suggests at least a 133 MHz Pentium processor for the installation of Office XP. In addition, you need the following:

- Windows 98, Me, XT, NT4, or 2000 Professional as the operating system. If you have Windows 95 or older you will need to upgrade your system!
- Random access memory (RAM) required is:

  For Windows 98, 24 MB plus 8 MB for each Office application running at the same time.

  For Windows Me or NT, 32 MB plus 8 MB for each Office application running at the same time.

- *For Windows 2000*, 64 MB plus 8 MB for each Office application running at the same time.
- Hard disc space required for the Professional edition of Office XP is 245 MB, but this varies with your system.
- CD-ROM drive.
- SuperVGA (800 x 600) or higher screen resolution with at least 256-colour display.
- Pointing device: Microsoft Mouse or compatible.

Realistically, to run Access 2002 and other Office XP applications, with reasonable sized files, you will need the most powerful Pentium PC with at least 128 MB of RAM. To run Microsoft Office XP from a network, you must also have a network compatible with your Windows operating environment, such as Microsoft's Windows 98 or higher, Windows NT4, LAN Manager, etc.

Finally, if you are connected to the Internet, you can take advantage of the extra help located on Microsoft's Web sites, or use Access's Internet facilities.

Installing Microsoft Office XP

Installing Office XP on your computer is done with the Setup program, located on the program CD-ROM.

Note: If you are using a virus detection utility, disable it before running Setup, as it might conflict with it.

To install Microsoft Office XP, place the distribution CD in your CD drive and close it. The auto-start program on the CD will start the Setup program automatically. If that does not work, click the **Start** button, and select the **Run** command which opens the Run dialogue box, shown in Fig. 1.3 on the next page.

Next, type in the **Open** text box:

```
G:\setup
```

as shown here.

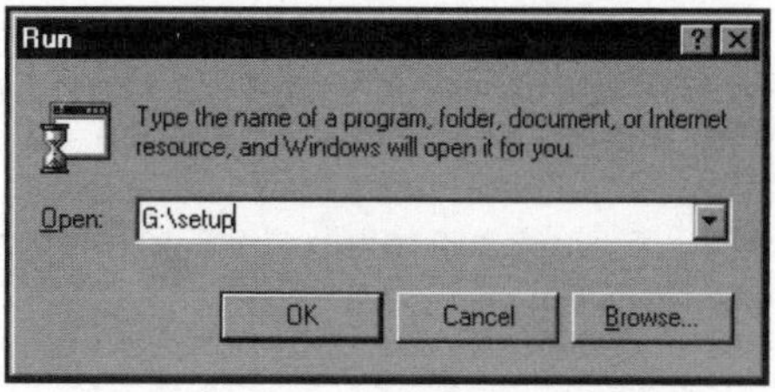

Fig. 1.3 Using the Windows Run Box

In this case we used the CD-ROM in the G: drive; yours could well be a different drive. Clicking the **OK** button, starts the installation of Microsoft Office XP. Setup displays the first of several screens.

We suggest that you follow the instructions displayed on the screen. With us Setup went through the following procedure:

You are prompted to type your name and the name of your organisation (optional) and then the 25-character Product Key for your version of the program. If you haven't found this it is on the back of the CD case. Then move to the second box by pressing the **Next** button. You are then asked to accept the licence agreement and passed to the box shown here in Fig. 1.4.

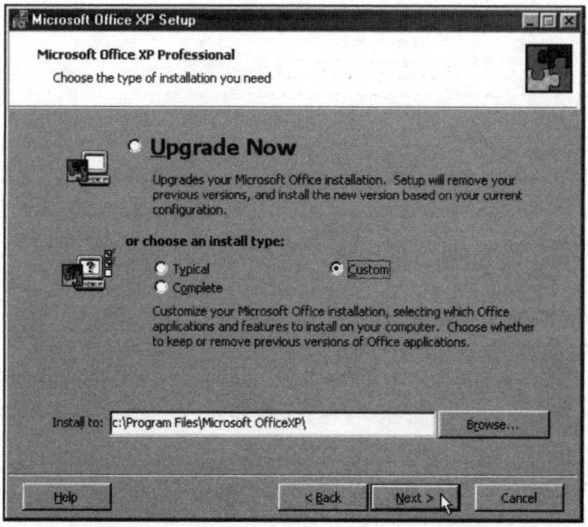

Fig. 1.4 Selecting the Type of Installation

If you are happy to do it, the easiest way is to select the default **Upgrade Now** option. But if, like us, you want to make sure everything works before losing your previous version of Office, we suggest you select the **Custom** option and enter a new folder destination to hold the new package. Obviously to do this you will need extra hard disc space, but with modern machines that should not be too much of a problem.

In the next box select the Office applications you want to install and click the **Choose detailed installation options for each application** option, before clicking on **Next**.

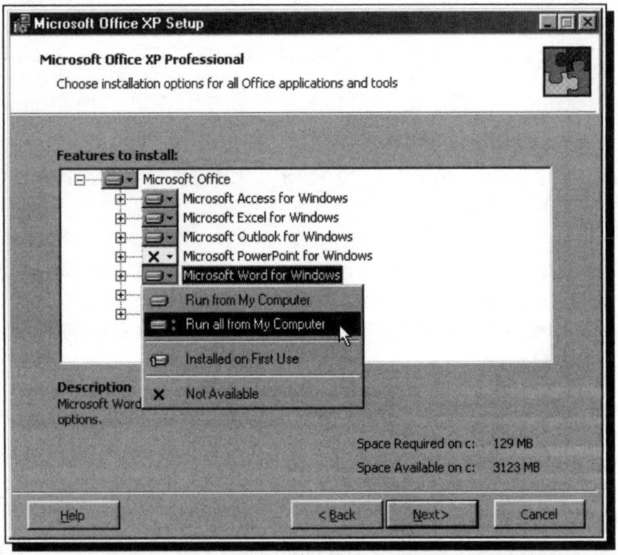

Fig. 1.5 Selecting the Features to Install

The next box, shown in Fig. 1.5 above, lets you select exactly the features you want for each application. If this looks a little confusing, we suggest you click the **Help** button to access the Office Setup Help System which will explain all the features here, as shown in our Fig. 1.6 on the next page.

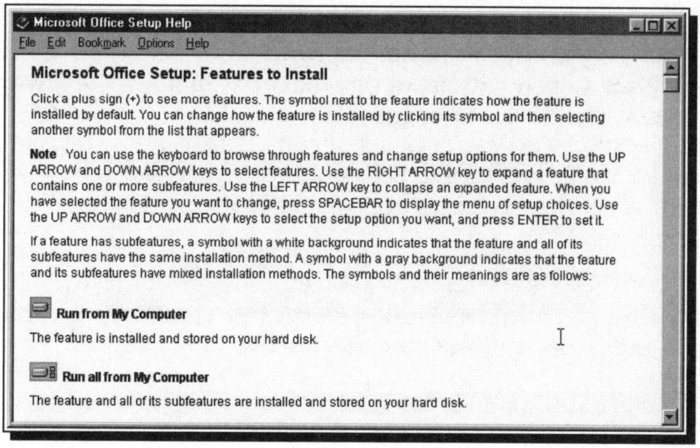

Fig. 1.6 An Office Setup Help Window

To avoid having to use the Office CD every time you want to use one of the extra Access features we suggest you make sure that all the options under Microsoft Access are set to **Run from My Computer**.

The next box (not shown here) lets you choose which older Office programs you want to keep on your PC (if any). You do not get the choice with Outlook, as the new Outlook 2002 is 'mandatory'.

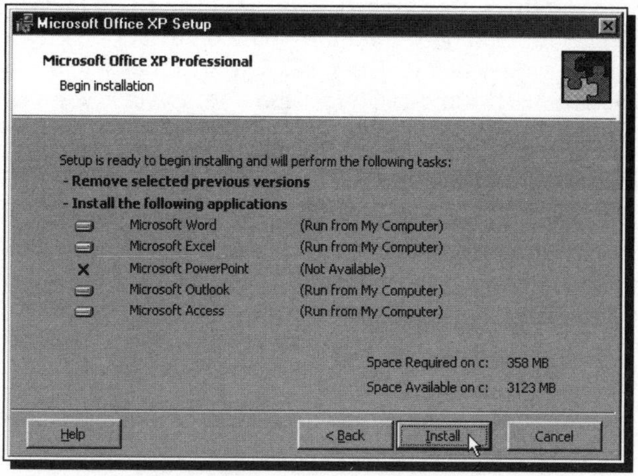

Fig. 1.7 Check List for the Installation

The next dialogue box (Fig. 1.7) lists what will be removed and installed. If you are not happy with anything here, press the **Back** button and make any required changes. Otherwise press **Install** to start the operation.

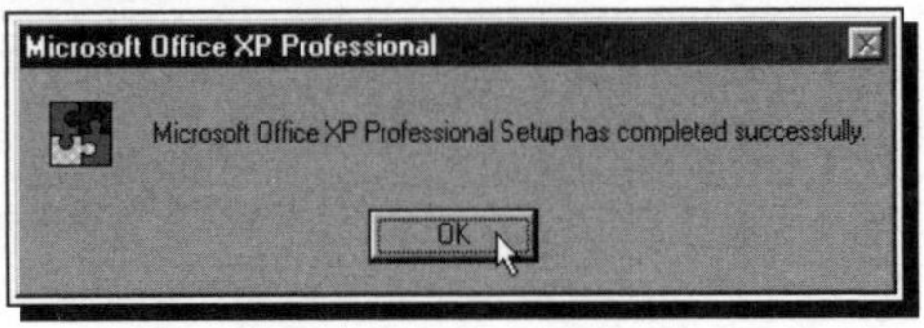

Fig. 1.8 Finished at Last!

Hopefully you will eventually be presented with the message box shown in Fig. 1.8. We found it worth the effort though.

The Setup program modifies your system files automatically so that you can start Access easily by creating and displaying a new entry in the **Start, Programs** cascade menu.

In addition, Office XP adds two entries to the top section of the Windows **Start** menu; the **New Office Document**, and the **Open Office Document**. The first allows you to select in a displayed dialogue box the tab containing the type of document you want to work with, with Access this will be **Databases**. Double-clicking the template you want, automatically starts Access.

The second entry allows you to work with existing files, or databases. Opening a database, first starts Access, then opens the database in it.

Activating Your Software

In an effort to restrict the 'illegal' use of their software, Microsoft have introduced an activation procedure with Office XP. You can only use it more than fifty times if you complete this activation procedure by phone, or over the Internet. It also means that, in theory, you can only use XP on one machine. Perhaps times are getting harder at Microsoft. When you first open Access 2002 you may be presented with the box shown in Fig. 1.9.

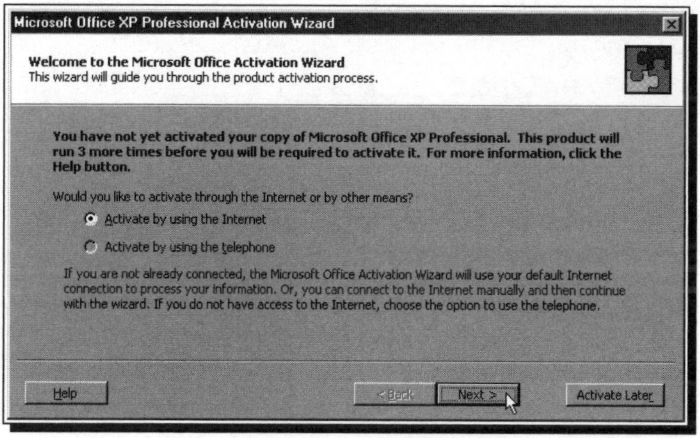

Fig. 1.9 The Activation Wizard

If so, you will have to follow the Wizard's instructions. We found the easiest way was to log on to the Internet and then work through the five dialogue boxes that were presented. The only information that was essential was the country we were using the software in.

Apparently the activation procedure marries up the product key details of the software with the hardware setup of your computer. This makes a unique combination, and Microsoft will not let that software be activated on another computer at the same time. In fact, if you re-format your hard disc, or change your hardware installation too much, you will have to re-activate the software. The only consolation is that the procedure is fairly quick and painless.

Adding or Removing Office Applications

To add or remove an Office application, left-click the Windows **Start** button at the bottom left corner of the screen, point to **Settings**, then click the **Control Panel** option on the Windows pop-up menu.

This opens the Control Panel dialogue box. Next, double-click the Add/Remove Programs icon, shown here to the left, to open the dialogue box shown in Fig. 1.10 below. Click the Install/Uninstall tab and select the Microsoft Office XP program, and then click the **Add/Remove** button.

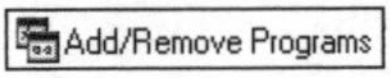

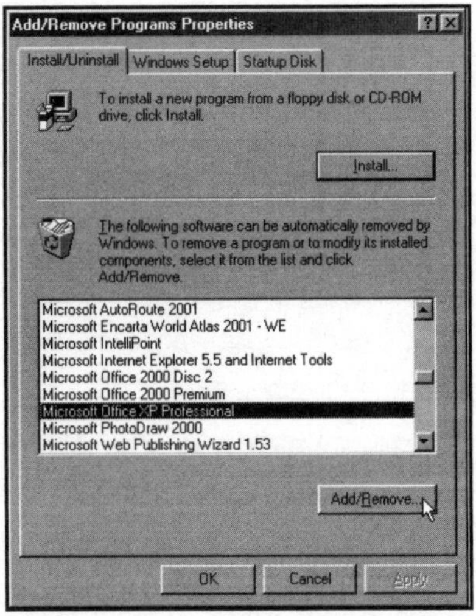

Fig. 1.10 The Add/Remove Programs Box

Office Setup will then display the Maintenance Mode dialogue box shown overleaf in Fig. 1.11. You will need to insert the Office XP CD into your CD drive to carry out most of the functions offered.

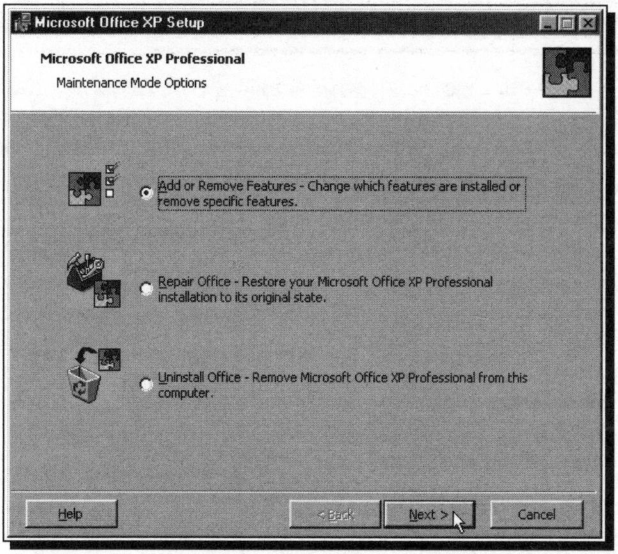

Fig. 1.11 Office XP Maintenance Mode Dialogue Box

Selecting **Add or Remove Features** opens up the dialogue box shown in Fig. 1.5 in which you can select which Office applications and features you want installed.

Note the additional buttons on the above screen. Use the **Repair Office** button to reinstall the whole of Office XP, or to find and fix any errors in your original installation.

Finally, you can use the **Uninstall Office** button to uninstall all of the Office XP applications.

New Features in Access 2002

Like other Microsoft Office XP applications, Access 2002 has a cleaner, simpler look to its interface. To quote Microsoft, “Softer colours help contribute to an updated feel”. Other changes include:

Task panes - Some of the most common tasks in Access are now organised in panes that display alongside your working area. You can, for instance, quickly create new databases or open existing ones using the task pane that appears when you start Access, or continue working while you search for a file using the Search task pane, or pick from a gallery of items to paste in the Office Clipboard task pane.

Ask a Question box - When you want help you can type a question in this new box, located on the menu bar, and get a list of Help choices.

Smart tags - New in-place buttons let you immediately adjust how information is pasted or how automatic changes are made by Access.

Updated Clip Organiser - (Formerly the Clip Gallery). Has hundreds of new clip art files and an easy task pane interface.

Save a Web page as a single file - A special Web archive file format is available which lets you save all the elements of a Web page, including text and graphics, into a single file.

Office Safe Mode - Office XP programs can now detect and isolate start-up problems. This lets you get round the problem, run Access in safe mode, and continue working.

Crash reporting tool - Diagnostic information about program crashes can be collected and sent to your IT department or to Microsoft itself, allowing problems to be corrected in the easiest way.

PivotChart and PivotTable Views - Access 2002 introduces PivotTable and PivotChart views to tables, queries, views, stored procedures, functions, and forms. These views can be saved as data access pages that can be viewed by anyone who has Microsoft Internet Explorer 5 or later.

XML Support - XML (Extensible Markup Language) is a technology for interchanging data on the Web, and for exchanging data between business software applications. Access 2002 provides powerful support for XML.

Extended Support with Microsoft SQL Server 2000 - By using extended properties in your Access 2002 projects, you can implement such features as lookup relationships, validation rules (or constraints), text formatting, and subdatasheets. These are getting a little advanced for the present book!

Interchangeable file format with Access 2000 - allows you to easily share different versions of database files with other Access users.

Multiple Undo and Redo - You now have the ability to undo and redo multiple actions in Design view in all objects of an Access database and in views, stored procedures, and functions in an Access project.

Updateable Off-line Data Access Pages - You can now take the data access pages in your Access project off-line, make changes to them (on a laptop say), and have them automatically synchronize when you reconnect to the SQL server.

Subforms/Subreports have improvements in Design view.

Linked Table Wizard - This can guide you through the process of linking Access tables to a SQL Server database from within an Access project.

Improved Accessibility Features - Access 2002 now provides even greater ease in working with forms and reports.

- Pressing **F8** in form or report Design view now displays the field list.
- Pressing <Enter> after selecting a field in the field list in form or report Design view will automatically add the field to the form or report design surface.
- Pressing <Ctrl+Tab> will move the focus from a form or report section to a subsection.

- Two additional powers (1,000% and 500%) have been added to the Zoom option in the print preview feature.

2

The Access Environment

Starting Access

There are several ways to start the Access program. You can click the Windows **Start** button, select **Programs** and then click on the 'Microsoft Access' entry in the cascade menu, as shown in Fig. 2.1 below.

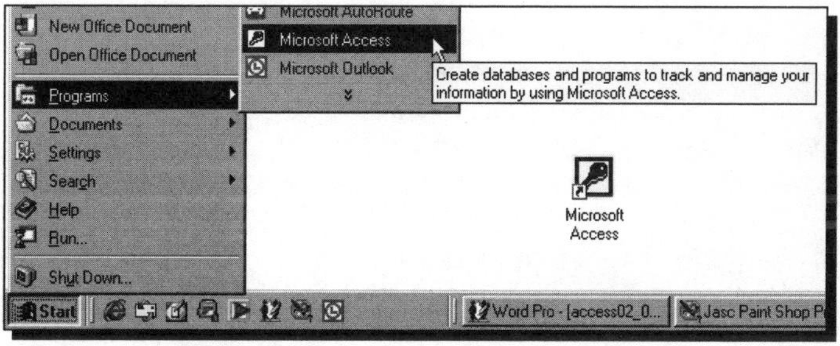

Fig. 2.1 The Windows Start Menu System

When it is installed, Office XP adds two entries to the top section of the Windows **Start** menu; **New Office Document**, and **Open Office Document** as shown above. These can be used to create new Access databases and to open existing ones as explained on page 8. Also just double-clicking on an Access database file in a 'My Computer' window will open Access with the database loaded.

Our favourite method is to create a shortcut on the Windows desktop, as shown in Fig. 2.1. This is easily done by highlighting the Access entry in the cascade menu, as shown above, dragging the pointer to the desktop with the right mouse button depressed, and selecting the **Create Shortcut(s) Here** option when the button is released. Double-clicking this shortcut 'icon' will open Access.

Task Panes

Some of the common tasks in Access 2002 can now be carried out in new task panes that display on the right side of the Access window. You can quickly create new databases or open files using the New File task pane that appears when you first start the program. The Search task pane gives you easy access to Windows' file search facilities, or you can visually pick from a gallery of items in the Office Clipboard task pane.

Fig. 2.2 shows the New File task pane with its control buttons on top. The left and right arrows let you quickly move between the task panes you have open, the down arrow opens a drop-down list of the available tasks, as shown here. The x button lets you close the pane. To re-open it, either click the New toolbar button, or right-click in the toolbar area and select **Task Pane** from the shortcut menu that is opened.

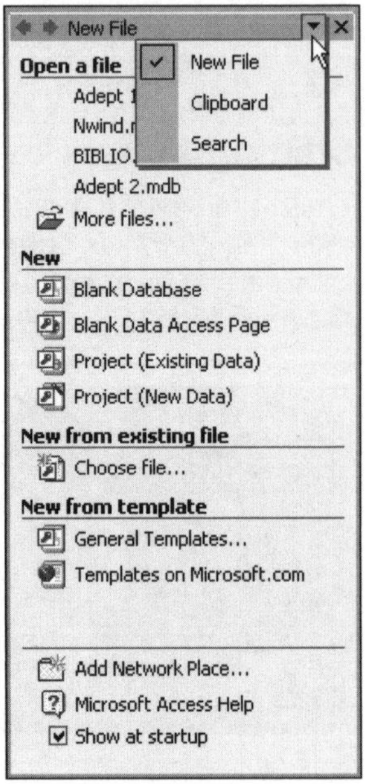

Fig. 2.2
The Task Pane List

We must admit to having reservations about this new feature of Office XP, but at times task panes can make some of the program features much easier and quicker to access. Each type of pane will be discussed in more detail as they are encountered throughout the book.

Access 2000 makes extensive use of Wizards, which have been designed to help the new user to create databases more easily. In particular, the Database Wizard builds the necessary elements for over 20 different databases for both home and business use. All you have to do is to answer a set of questions and the Wizard builds the database for you.

Parts of the Access Screen

Before we start designing a database, let us take a look at a typical Access 2002 opening screen.

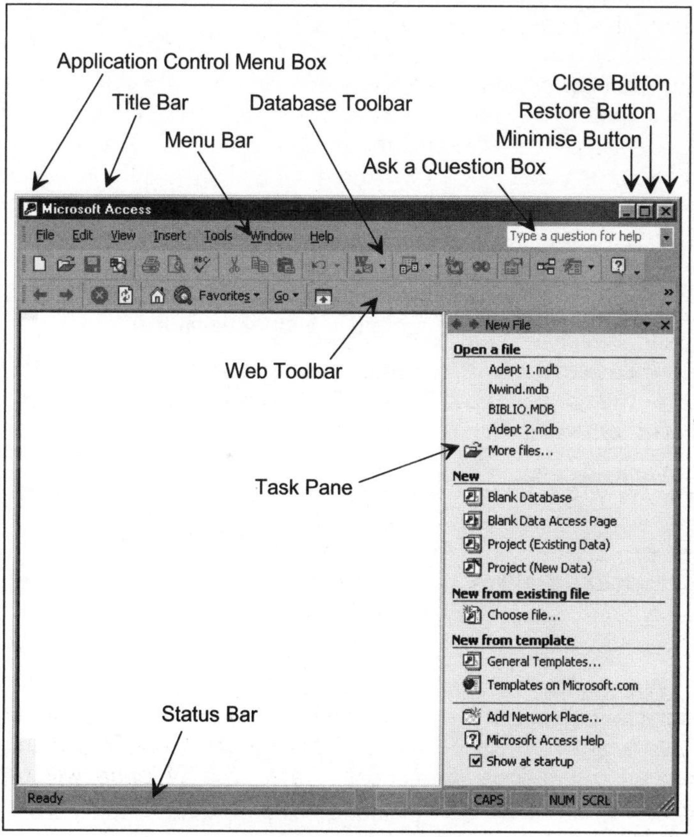

Fig. 2.3 The Access Screen Layout

As you can see, these windows have common screen elements with those of other Microsoft Office applications. As usual, depending on what you are doing with Access, the items on the menu bar can be different from those of the opening screen. Although more than one window can be displayed simultaneously, only one is the active window (which normally displays on top of any other non-active windows. Title bars of non-active windows appear a lighter shade than those of the active one. To activate another window, click with the left mouse button anywhere within it.

The various screen areas have the following functions:

Area	***Function***
Command button	Clicking on this button,  (see upper-left corner of the Access window), displays a pull-down menu which can be used to control the program window. It includes commands for restoring, moving, sizing, maximising, minimising, and closing the window.
Title bar	The bar at the top of a window which displays the application name.
Minimise box	When clicked, this button  minimises the application to the Windows Taskbar.
Restore button	Clicking on this button  restores the active window to the position and size that was occupied before it was maximised. The Restore button is then  replaced by a Maximise button, shown here, which can then be used to set the window to full screen size.
Close button	The extreme top right  button that you click to close a window.

Menu bar	The bar below the Title bar which allows you to choose from several menu options. Clicking on a menu item displays the pull-down menu associated with that item. The options listed in the Menu bar depend on what you are doing at the time, as well as your recent activities.
Ask a Question Box	The text box at the far right of the menu bar. You can type in a help query and press the Return key to get a listing of matching topics.
Toolbars	The bars below the Menu bar which contain buttons that give you mouse click access to the most often used functions in the program, as well as to Internet Web sites from within Access
Task Pane	A new pane which presents controls on the right-hand side of the screen. It has its own button bar for instant control.
Status Bar	The bottom line of the window that displays status and other useful information.

The Menu Bar Options

Each window's menu bar option has associated with it a pull-down sub-menu. To activate the menu of a window, either press the <Alt> key, which highlights the first option of the menu (usually **File**), then use the right and left arrow keys to highlight any of the options in the menu, or use the mouse to point to an option. Pressing either the <Enter> key, or the left mouse button, reveals the pull-down sub-menu of the highlighted menu option.

The sub-menu of the **File** option of the Access window, is shown below.

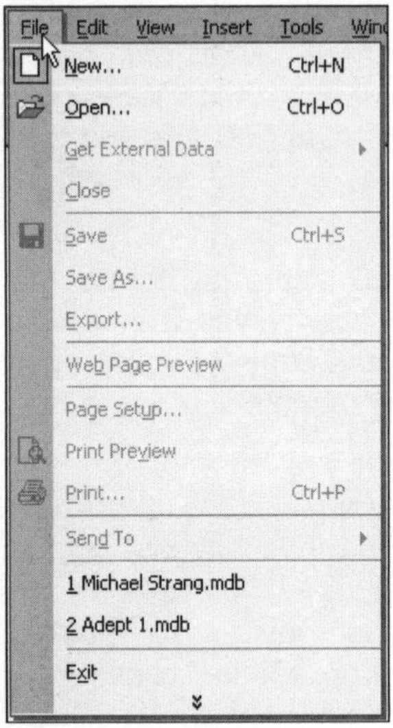

Fig. 2.4 The File Sub-menu

Menu options can also be activated directly by pressing the <Alt> key followed by the underlined letter of the required option. Thus pressing **Alt+F**, displays the pull-down sub-menu of **File** as shown.

You can use the up and down arrow keys to move the highlighted bar up and down a sub-menu, or the right and left arrow keys to move along the options in the menu bar. Pressing the <Enter> key selects the highlighted option or executes the highlighted command. Pressing the <Esc> key once, closes the pull-down sub-menu, while pressing the <Esc> key for a second time, closes the menu system.

Depending on what you are doing with Access, different menu and sub-menu options are available or become active. Access 2002 also automatically personalises both menus and toolbars based on how often you use particular commands. With toolbars this only becomes apparent when you are using a small window size, which is not big enough to hold all the available toolbar buttons.

When you first start the program, the most basic commands appear. Then, as you work, Access adjusts the menus and toolbars so that only the commands and toolbar buttons you use most often appear. To find a command you don't use often, or have never used before, click the arrows at the bottom of the menu to expand it to show all the options available, as shown in Fig 2.5 on the next page.

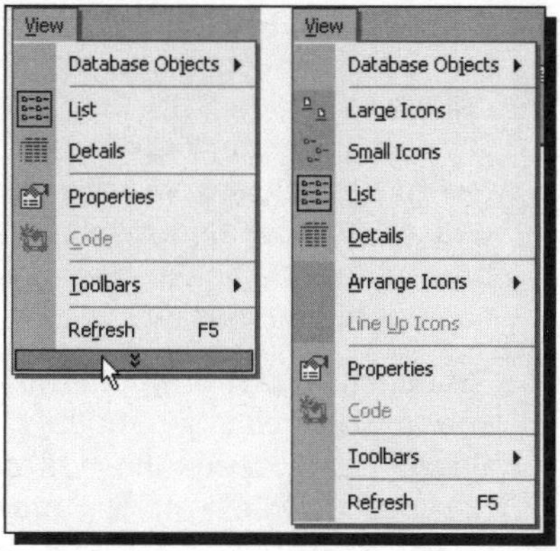

Fig. 2.5 Short and Full Versions of the View Menu

This shows the 'default' **View** menu on the left, and the same menu fully expanded on the right. Any options not available at the time appear in a lighter shade of grey.

You can also double-click a menu item to expand its sub-menu. When you expand one menu, all of the other menus are also expanded until you choose a command or perform another action.

When you click a command on the expanded menu, it is immediately added to the personalised menu. It is dropped from the personalised menu again if you use Access several times without using that command.

In general, Access 2002 menu options offer the following:

File Produces a pull-down menu of mainly file related tasks, such as creating a **New** database, the ability to **Open**, or **Close** database files, to **Get External Data** from other databases, and **Save** database files with the same name, or **Save As** a different name, or to **Export** into different file formats. You can **Search** for files, use **Page Setup** to set the margins and the size of your printed page, **Print Preview** a table, form, or query on screen before committing it to paper, or **Print** it to paper. You can use the **Send To** option to attach a particular database feature to an e-mail, or view **Database Properties**. Finally, you can **Exit** the program. Above this last sub-menu option, Access also displays the names of the last four databases you used so that you can open them easily.

Edit Produces a pull-down menu which allows you to **Undo** changes made, **Cut**, **Copy** and **Paste** text, open the **Office Clipboard** pane, and **Delete** or **Rename** a database object. Lets you **Create Shortcuts** to database objects, as well as managing database **Groups**.

View This menu, shown on the previous page, gives you control over what you see on the screen. For example, you can choose to view several database objects, such as tables, queries, forms, etc., and view files as icons or lists. You can also select which toolbars you want to be displayed.

Insert Allows you to insert tables, queries, forms, reports, pages, macros, or modules. You can even use **AutoForm** and **AutoReport** to create forms and reports automatically.

Tools Allows you to spell-check your work, switch on the AutoCorrect facility, use Office links, or open a Microsoft Netmeeting. You can also add or change relationships between database tables, analyse features of your database, use an extensive range of utilities, specify the level of security required, run or create Visual Basic macros, customise the way Access operates for you and generally control its option settings.

Window Allows you to display multiple windows on the screen in 'cascade' or 'tile' form, to arrange icons within an active window, or to hide or redisplay the active window.

Help Activates the help menu which you can use to access **Microsoft Access Help**, to display the Office Assistant, to use the **What's This**? facility described below, or the **Office on the Web** option (if you are connected to the Internet). You can activate the application, if you ever need to start this process yourself, open **Sample Databases**, **Detect and Repair** some Access problems, or use the **About Microsoft Access** option to get details of your version of Access and your operating system.

For a more detailed description of each sub-menu item, click **What's This** on the **Help** menu and the pointer will change to a question mark, as shown here. Clicking with this on the menu item you want information about opens a small text box of help, as shown below in Fig. 2.6.

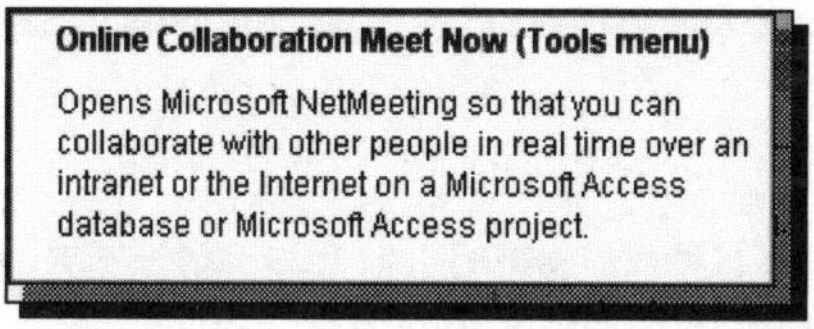

Online Collaboration Meet Now (Tools menu)
Opens Microsoft NetMeeting so that you can collaborate with other people in real time over an intranet or the Internet on a Microsoft Access database or Microsoft Access project.

Fig. 2.6 'What's This' Help on a Menu Item

When an object, such as a table, is open, additional main menu options are displayed. With a table for example, the **Format** and **Records** menu options are available.

Shortcut Menus

To see a shortcut menu containing the most common commands applicable to an item, point with your mouse at the item and click the right mouse button. For example, left-clicking the adjacent **Open** toolbar button, displays the Open dialogue box. Right-clicking within the 'empty' area of this dialogue box, displays the short-cut menu shown below:

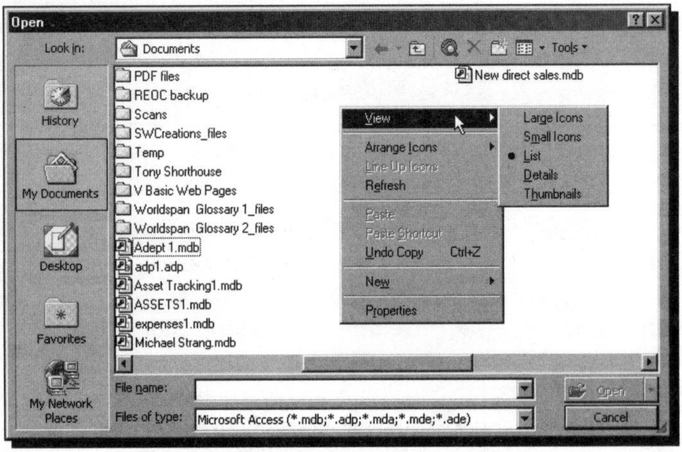

Fig. 2.7 Using Right-click Shortcut Menus

In this case we have the option to **View** the contents of the logged folder (Documents) in five different ways. In our example above we are using the **List** view, which we find easier to work with. You can actually carry out much of your file management in this Open dialogue box, as right-clicking on file or folder names opens shortcut menus to let you manipulate them.

Having activated a shortcut menu, you can close it without taking any further action by simply pressing the <Esc> key.

If you haven't used these shortcut menus before we strongly recommend you start now, as they can save you a lot of time.

The Toolbars

There are two common toolbars available in Access 2002, the Database toolbar and the Web toolbar. If they are not open you can use the **View**, **Toolbars** menu command, or more easily, right-click in the toolbar area, to open ther special shortcut menu shown here. In this list active bars are shown with a blue tick to their left. Clicking on a list entry will toggle that toolbar on or off.

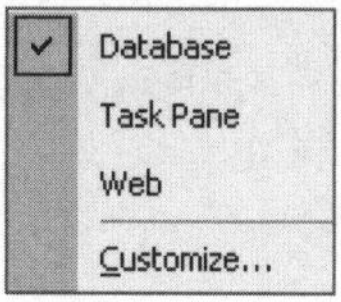

If you are working with a small window, or screen size, not all of the toolbar buttons (or icons) will be visible. To see the other available buttons click the toolbar options button at the right end of the bar, as shown in Fig. 2.8 below.

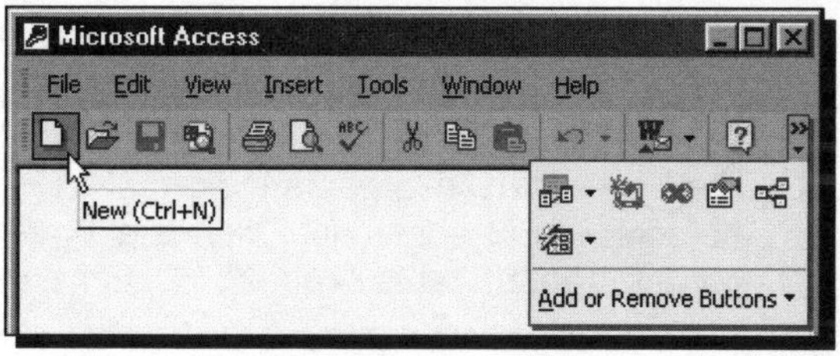

Fig. 2.8 Toolbar Options

Clicking any of the buttons now displayed will action that function. As can be seen you also have the option to **Add or Remove Buttons** and customise your toolbar yourself.

To 'complicate' matters further, Access automatically customises both toolbars and menus, based on how often you use their commands. As you work, they adjust so that only the buttons and commands you use most often are shown. Thus you may not see exactly the same features displayed on your screen, as shown here.

To see the function of a toolbar button, move the pointer over it until it 'activates'. A banner with its name will then appear, as shown on the left of Fig. 2.8. To carry out that function you simply left-click on the button.

The Mouse Pointers

In Microsoft Access, as with all other graphical based programs, using a mouse makes many operations both easier and more fun to carry out.

Access 2002 makes use of the mouse pointers available in Windows, some of the most common of which are illustrated below. When Access is initially started up the first you will see is the hourglass, which turns into an upward pointing hollow arrow once the individual application screen appears on your display. Other shapes depend on the type of work you are doing at the time.

The hourglass which displays when you are waiting while performing a function.

The arrow which appears when the pointer is placed over menus, scrolling bars, and buttons.

The I-beam which appears in normal text areas of the screen. For additional 'Click and Type' pointer shapes, see the table overleaf.

The 4-headed arrow which appears when you choose to move a table, a chart area, or a frame.

The double arrows which appear when over the border of a window, used to drag the side and alter the size of the window.

The Help hand which appears in the Help windows, and is used to access 'hypertext' type links, (with the <Ctrl> key depressed).

Access 2002, like other Windows packages, has additional mouse pointers which facilitate the execution of selected commands. Some of these have the following functions:

The vertical pointer which appears when pointing over a column in a table or worksheet and used to select the column.

The horizontal pointer which appears when pointing at a row in a table or worksheet and used to select the row.

The slanted arrow which appears when the pointer is placed in the selection bar area of text or a table.

The vertical split arrow which appears when pointing over the area separating two columns and used to size a column.

The horizontal split arrow which appears when pointing over the area separating two rows and used to size a row.

The cross which you drag to extend or fill a series.

The draw pointer which appears when you are drawing freehand.

Access has a few additional mouse pointers to the ones above, but their shapes are mostly self-evident.

Getting Help in Access

No matter how experienced you are, there will always be times when you need help to find out how to do something in Access 2002. It is after all a very large and powerful package with a multitude of features. As in previous versions of Access the much maligned Office Assistant, or Clippy as he is called by Microsoft, is still available, but by default it is switched off. It is also possible to install Access 2002 without the Assistant, if the option is not selected in the Setup box we showed in Fig. 1.5. As we shall see, there are several ways to get help now.

The Ask a Question Box

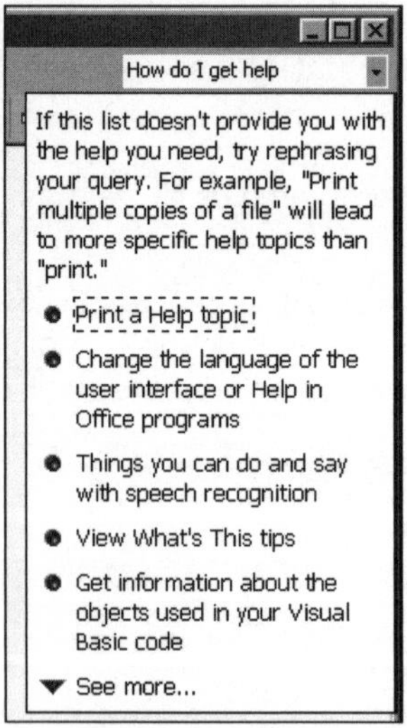

Fig. 2.9
The Ask a Question Box

To quickly access Help, you can use the new Ask a Question box on the menu bar. You type a question in this box, as we show in Fig. 2.9, and press the Enter key.

A list of help topics is then displayed, as shown here. To see more topics, left-click the small triangle at the bottom of the list with the caption 'See more'. Once you select an option from the list and click on it, the Help system is opened and you should quickly be able to find the answers you need. In fact it works the same way as the Assistant, but without the constant 'distractions'.

It is better to type a full question in the box, rather than just a keyword. The options presented can then be more relevant. When you use the feature several times, the previous questions can be accessed by clicking the down arrow to the right of the text box.

The Office Assistant

The Office Assistant is turned off by default in this version of Access and may not even be installed unless you specifically request it. When activated, it first appears as we show on the left, and automatically provides Help topics and tips on tasks you perform as you work. To find out how it works, start Access and use the **Help**, **Show the Office Assistant** menu command. This should open Clippy. Now just click him with the left mouse button, to open the 'What would you like to do?' box, shown in Fig. 2.10.

Fig. 2.10
Using the Office Assistant

To get help you simply type your query here and click the **Search** button. From then on the procedure is the same as with the Ask a Question box.

If you like, you can customise the Assistant, and decide if you want it to automatically display tips, messages, and alerts, make sounds, move when it's in the way, and guess a Help topic that it thinks you

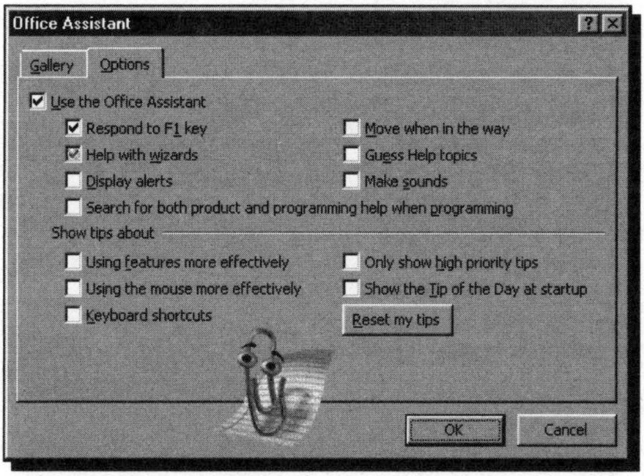

Fig. 2.11 The Office Assistant Options Box

may need. You can also switch it off once you have mastered a particular Office application, or cannot cope with its intrusions any more! All of these features are controlled from the box shown in Fig. 2.11 which is opened by clicking the **Options** button shown in Fig. 2.10.

To change the shape of your Office Assistant (there are eight shapes to choose from), either left-click the Gallery tab of the dialogue box shown in Fig. 2.11, or right-click the Office Assistant and select the **Choose Assistant** option from the displayed menu, as shown here in Fig. 2.12.

Fig. 2.12 Shortcut Menu

Either of these actions displays the following dialogue box (Fig. 2.13) in which you can select your preferred Assistant shape by left-clicking the **Next** button.

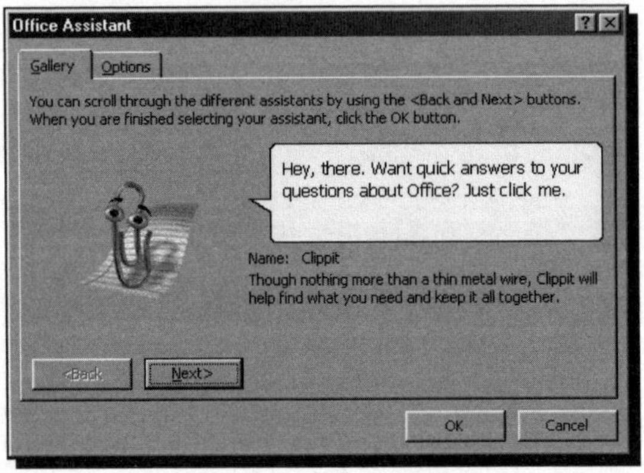

Fig. 2.13 The Office Assistant Gallery Box

The eight shapes of the available Assistants are shown in Fig. 2.14 on the next page. We find the Office Assistant's animated characters to be very clever and amusing, but must admit that like most people we prefer to work with the facility turned off. To do this, make sure the **Use the Office Assistant** option is not selected in the Options box shown in Fig. 2.11.

Clippit	The Dot	F1

Merlin	Office Logo	Mother Nature

Links	Rocky	

Fig. 2.14 The Office Assistant Shapes

The Main Help System

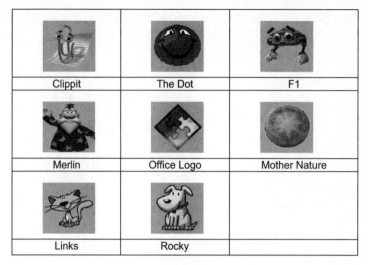

If you turn the Office Assistant completely off (as described on the last page) and press the **F1** function key, or click the **Help** toolbar button shown here, or use the **Help**, **Microsoft Access Help** menu command, Help will be accessed directly through the Help window. This is the way we prefer to use it.

When first opened, the Microsoft Access Help Center will be displayed in the right-hand pane as shown in Fig. 2.15 on the next page. This gives a quick way to get information on **What's New** with Access 2002, the **Microsoft Office Web Site** and about **Getting Help** itself. Each of these has a very colourful button you can press.

Below these is a listing of 'hypertext links' to some of the help topics Microsoft thought you were most likely to use first. Clicking any of these opens the relevant Help page, without you having to look for the item itself.

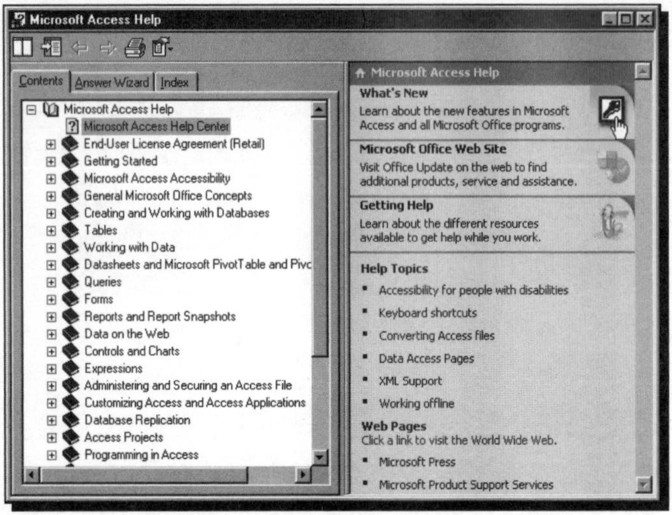

Fig. 2.15 Microsoft Access Help

As can be seen here, the left pane of the Help window has three tabbed sections.

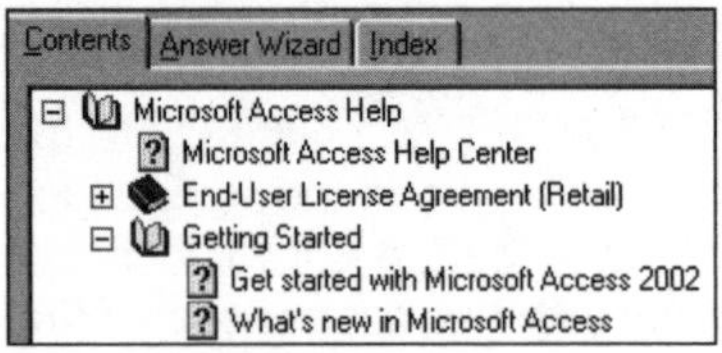

Fig. 2.16 Help Contents List

The **Contents** tab of the Help screen opens up an impressive list of topics relating to the Access 2002 program. Clicking a '+' at the left of an item, or double-clicking a closed book icon, opens a sub-list; clicking a '—', or double-clicking an open book icon, will close it again. Clicking a list item, with the ? mark as shown, opens the help text in the right-hand pane.

To type a question in the Help window, you click the **Answer Wizard** tab. When you want to search for specific words or phrases, you click the **Index** tab.

For example, click the **Answer Wizard** tab, and type the text *How do I open a database* in the **What would you like to do?** text box. Then click the **Search** button and you should see something like the following.

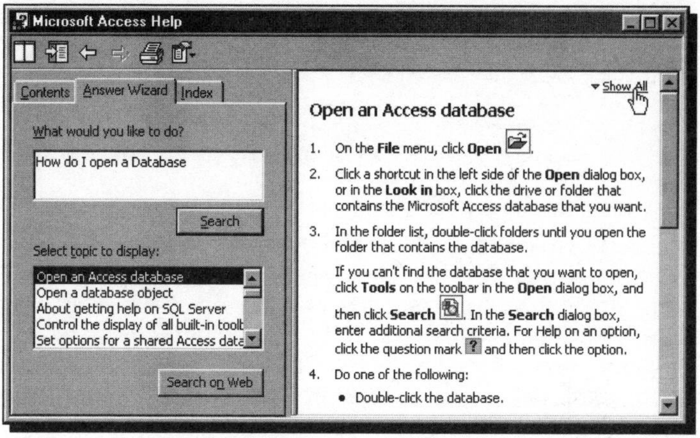

Fig. 2.17 Using the Help Answer Wizard

Clicking an item in the list of topics opens the relevant Help page in the right pane. A new feature with Office XP is that the Help pages are opened in an 'outline' view. Clicking a blue link item with a ▸ symbol to its left, opens up more detail, whereas clicking the ▾ **Show All** link in the top-right corner will fully expand the page. This is very useful if you want to print or copy the Help information.

The Help Toolbar

You can control the Help window with the six buttons on the toolbar, as follows:

Auto Tile - Tiles the Help window on the screen next to the main Access window.

Hide - Closes and re-opens the left half of the Help window, giving more room for the Help text.

Back - Opens the last Help page viewed in the current session list.

Forward - Opens the next Help page viewed in the current session list.

Print - prints either the current page, or all of the topics in the selected heading.

Options - gives a sub-menu of all the other toolbar options, as well as allowing you to hide the Help tabs.

The Access Help system is quite comprehensive but it is not always easy to find the information you are looking for. It sometimes pays to select the feature, or object, you want details on before accessing Help, you may then get exactly the right information straight off. Do spend some time here to learn, particularly what is new in Access. Other topics can always be explored later.

ScreenTips

If you want to know what a menu command or button does, or if you want to know more about an option in a dialogue box, you can also get ScreenTips help. These can be accessed in three ways:

- For help with a menu command, toolbar icon, or a screen region, click **What's This?** on the **Help** menu, or <Shift + F1>, and then click the feature you want help on.
- In a dialogue box, click the Help icon  in the top right corner of the box, and then click the option.
- To see the name of a toolbar button, rest the pointer over the button and its name will appear.

Help on the Internet

If all else fails, you can connect to several Microsoft Web sites with the **Help**, **Office on the Web** menu command. You must obviously have an Internet connection for this to work, though!

3

Database Basics

Before we start designing a database using Access 2002, it would be a good idea to look at the various elements that make up a database. To do so, start Access, which should open with the New File task pane active, as shown here in Fig. 3.1. If the task pane is not visible, click  the **New** toolbar button to open it.

Fig. 3.1
The New File Task Pane

Next, select the **Blank Database** option. This opens the File New Database dialogue box (shown in Fig. 3.2 on the next page) for you to name and save the database file.

In the **File name** box, type the database name, **Adept 1** is the sample database we will be building in the next chapter, so we will use that name. We suggest you go along with us to fully benefit from the example. The new name then replaces the default name **db1**. Access adds the extension **.mdb** automatically so you don't have to worry too much about it. In our example we are saving the new database in the **2002 Examples** folder (a sub-folder in My Documents on our C: drive), but you can obviously save it wherever you like. The Places Bar, shown in the left of the box lets you quickly access many commonly used folders.

Finally, pressing the **Create** button creates the empty database and displays its Database window, as shown in Fig. 3.3 on the next page.

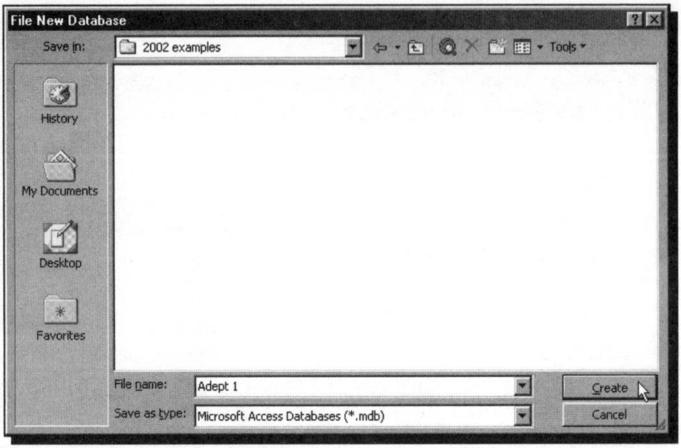

Fig. 3.2 The File New Database Box

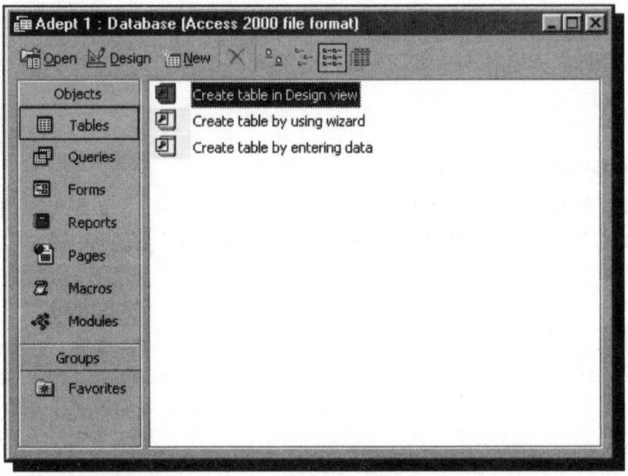

Fig. 3.3 The Database Window for our Empty Database

It is in this Database window that you can design the various elements that make up a database, such as tables, queries, forms, reports, pages, macros and modules, most of which we will examine in more detail in the rest of the book. The objects you add will appear in the Database window, so that you can select them and work with them.

Database Elements

The **Objects** area of the Database window displays the types of objects available in an Access 2002 database, these are:

Tables

As we saw earlier, a table consists of fields and records of data, and is a collection of related information similar to a small spreadsheet. You must have at least one table in a database, but you can have many more.

Queries

Queries allow you to find the information you want from your database. A query is set up to find the data that meets a specific set of criteria, or conditions.

Forms

Forms usually display one record at a time, and provide an easy, more visual, way to view, enter and edit the information in that record.

Reports

Reports are formatted documents that display specific information from the database. Calculations and summaries are often carried out in reports.

Pages

Pages let you put 'live' database information onto the Internet, or your company's Intranet. Other users can then access and modify the data.

Macros

Macros can help you to automate tasks that you perform frequently. They combine a series of actions (that each perform a particular operation) into one action, such as clicking a macro button. They can save a lot of time.

Modules

Modules are programs created in Visual Basic for Applications that let you control how your database works.

To get a first look at some of these objects we need an actual database that contains them. This is no problem with Access 2002, as you can use the Database Wizard to create a number of 'standard' types of databases. You simply choose the type that is suitable for the information you want to put in it. The Wizard then creates the new database, giving you options for customising it during the process, as we shall see in the next chapter.

For now we will simply create one of their standard databases to have something to play with, and to get a general idea about the workings of the Access package.

An Instant Database

If necessary, start Access 2002 and click on the General Templates option in the **New from template** section of the New File task pane to open the Templates dialogue box. Clicking the Databases tab should show the following:

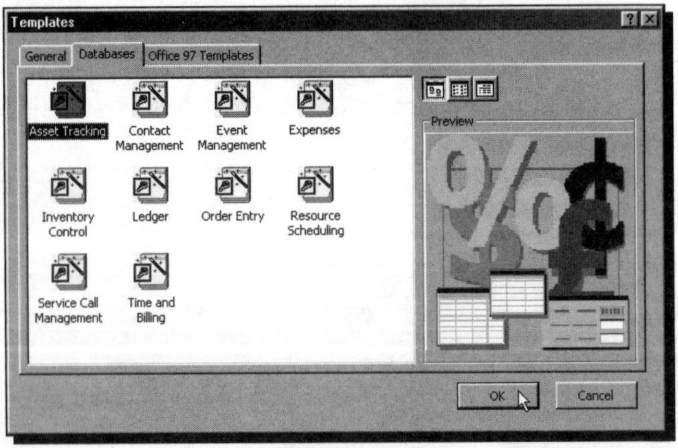

Fig. 3.4 The Ten Database Templates of Access 2002

The ten Access databases available to you are listed here. Unfortunately all of these are business orientated, if you want more personal ones you will have to look for them on Microsoft's Web site.

Select the Asset Tracking icon and click the **OK** button to start the procedure. Select the default name *Asset Tracking1.mdb,* unless you prefer something else, and click the **Create** button in the File New Database dialogue box. This generates an empty Database window and opens the Database Wizard, as shown in Fig. 3.5 below.

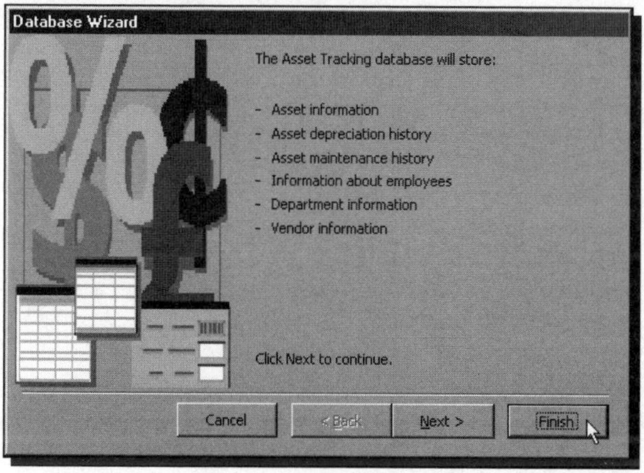

Fig. 3.5 The Database Wizard

After reading about the type of database that will be created, you have two choices. Clicking the **Next** button will step you through the Wizard, giving you customisation choices, while clicking the **Finish** button will create a database containing all the default elements.

For now, select **Finish** and wait for a couple of minutes while the new database objects are created. The Database window will then be reduced to an icon at the bottom of the screen, and the opening Main Switchboard window of the database will display, as shown in Fig. 3.6 on the next page.

A Switchboard is simply a menu of database options, and is actually one of the database forms, as we shall see in a later chapter.

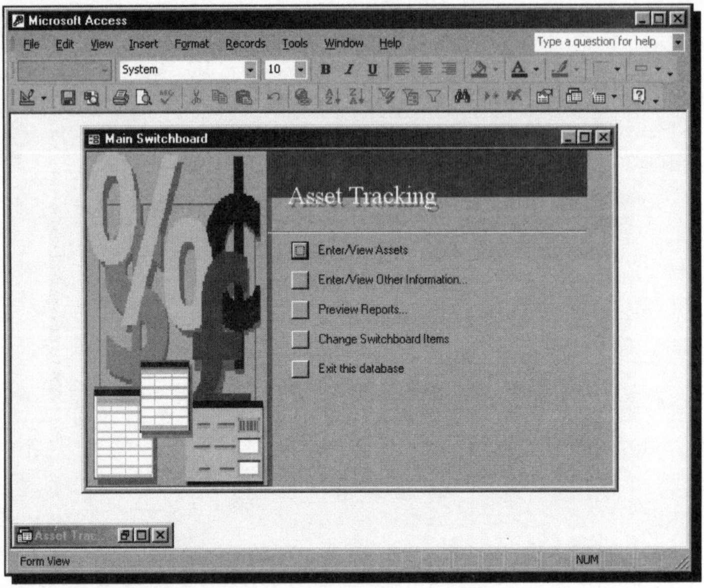

Fig. 3.6 The New Database Main Switchboard, or Menu

The Database Window

When you are ready, restore the Database window, by double-clicking on its minimised icon, by clicking the Database Window toolbar button shown here, or by pressing the **F11** key. It should look something like that in Fig. 3.7 on the next page.

Here 'Tables' is selected in the **Objects** bar, (or list), and the seven tables that make up this standard database are listed in the right-hand window pane. Selecting any of these and clicking the **Open** toolbar button will open that table, but there will not be any data in it. The whole database is empty, but it is ready to receive data.

Clicking the other Objects buttons in turn will show that there are also eleven forms, five reports and one module of code making up the database.

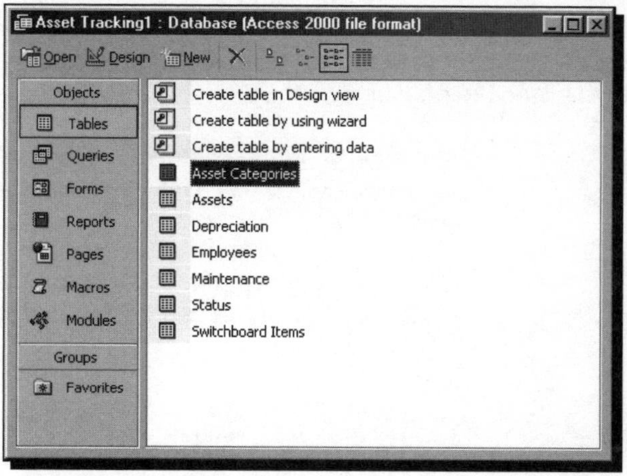

Fig. 3.7 The Database Window of the New Database

There are also options in each objects pane to start the procedure of creating a new object, such as 'Create table in Design view, by using wizard, or by entering data'. We shall see more of these procedures later.

The Database Window Toolbar

The buttons on this toolbar can save you a lot of time, so it is worth knowing their functions.

Opens the selected object in a view that lets you work with data. This is the same as double-clicking the object.

Opens the selected object in design view in which you can change the design and layout of the object.

Starts the procedure for creating a new object of the type selected.

Deletes the selected object, as long as it is not 'related' to another database object.

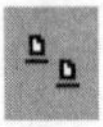

Displays objects as large icons.

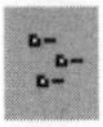

Displays objects as small icons.

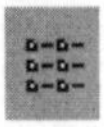

Displays objects in a list format - the display type we usually use.

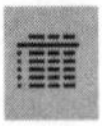

Displays extra details in the objects list.

You can change the design of any of the objects, or elements, of a database by selecting them and clicking the **Design** toolbar button shown above.

This is a good place to experiment a little with the objects of this 'trial' database, as you can always delete the database and start again if you come to grief!

Creating Groups

To make it easier to use a database you can create groups in which to keep related objects in the Database window. This way you could, for example, keep all the tables, forms and reports dealing with the same type of data in the same objects window pane.

To create a group, click the Groups bar in the **Objects** list, right-click in the area below, select **New Group** and name the group. When you want to add an object to the group, simply drag it from the right pane of the database window to the group name in the objects list. A very useful feature.

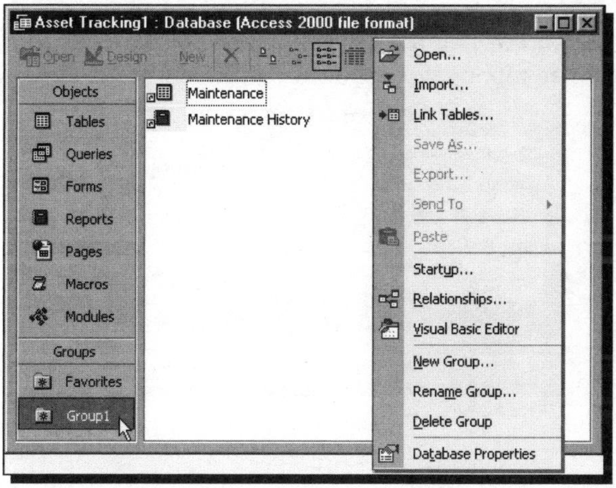

Fig. 3.8 A Database Group

In our example above we have created a group to hold the tables, forms and reports relating to 'Maintenance', but as you can see, we did not bother to rename it.

We also show above the shortcut menu that is opened when a Group button is right-clicked. Towards the bottom, this menu has three Group-related functions, including **Rename Group** and **Delete Group**.

Sample Databases with Access

Two complete sample databases were included with our version of Office XP. One of these, the Northwind database is well worth looking at to see how it has been constructed. You may well be able to modify it to your actual needs, or use parts of it at least.

The Northwind database contains the sales data for a company called Northwind Traders, which imports and exports speciality foods from around the world. Unfortunately Microsoft have not seen fit to include the other three database examples that were in previous versions of Access.

To open the Northwind database, use the **Help**, **Sample Databases** menu command, as shown in Fig. 3.9 below.

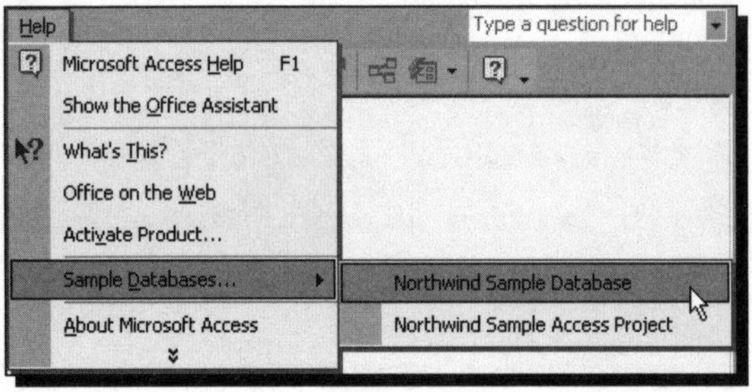

Fig. 3.9 Finding the Sample Databases

If the database was not installed with Access you will be given the option of installing it now. You will of course need the Office XP CD-ROM to do this.

Adding Access 2002 Features

If you want to add these sample databases manually, (or any other Office features), there is no problem as long as you have the CD-ROMs that were used for the original installation. If not, you will have to find them!

Place the Office XP disc in your CD-ROM drive and open the Windows Control Panel by selecting **Start**, **Settings**, **Control Panel**. Then double-click the Add/Remove Programs icon to open the dialogue box shown in Fig. 3.10.

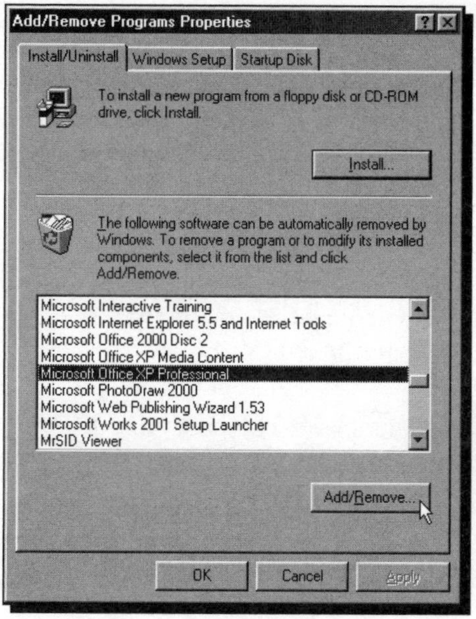

Fig. 3.10 The Windows Add/Remove Programs Box

Select the entry for your version of the program; in our case this was Microsoft Office XP Professional, but yours may be different, and click the **Add/Remove** button.

This opens the Office XP Maintenance Mode dialogue box which has options for adding and removing Office XP features, for repairing your Office installation, or if all else fails for un-installing Office XP from your computer.

Select the **Add or Remove Features** radio button and open the Microsoft Access for Windows list in the Microsoft Office XP Setup dialogue box, as shown in Fig. 3.11 on the next page.

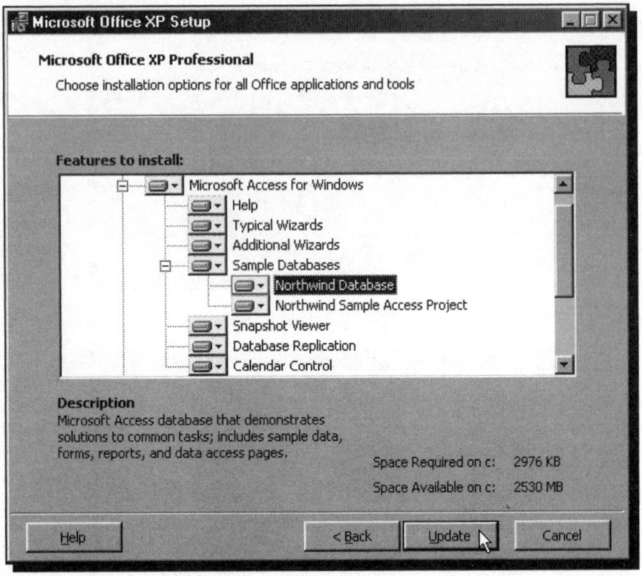

Fig. 3.11 Installing Extra Access Features

To install the sample databases, or other features, right-click the icon to the left of each one in turn and select **Run from my Computer** from the Shortcut menu. When all the Sample Database icons look like ours above, simply click the **Update** button to install them on your machine.

4

Creating our Database

Opening a Database

We will now get to grips with developing the database that we created and named **Adept 1** in the last chapter. Start Access and select Adept 1.mdb from the **Open a file** section of the New File task pane. If you don't want to use the task pane you can click the **Open** toolbar button, shown again here, and select the database file from the Open dialogue box (Fig. 2.7).

If you did not create this file before, just go back to the beginning of the previous chapter and do it now. It will only take a minute or two, and you will need it to benefit from what we will be doing.

Creating a Table

The easiest way to design a database table is by double-clicking the **Create table by using wizard** button in the Database window as shown here, which opens the Table Wizard dialogue box, of Fig. 4.2. The other options on the list, allow you to start designing a table from scratch in design view, or to have a table automatically created for you depending on the data you enter into it.

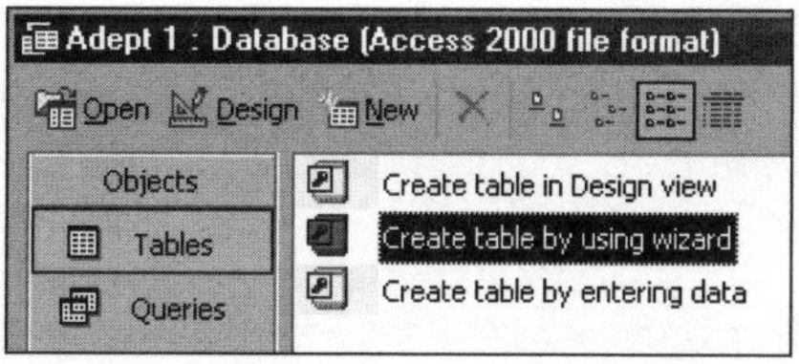

Fig. 4.1 Creating a Table with a Wizard

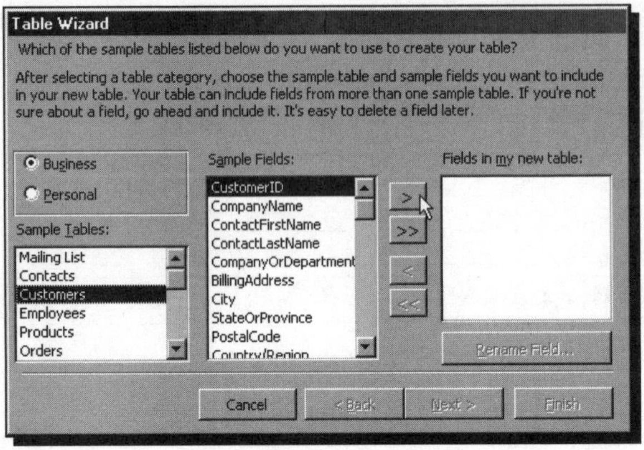

Fig. 4.2 The Table Wizard Window

The database we are going to create holds the invoicing details which the firm Adept Consultants keep on their clients. One table will hold the details of the clients, while another will hold the actual invoice details.

The wizard helps you very rapidly create a whole range of tables suitable for business or personal databases - we counted 45 in fact.

With **Business** checked, choose 'Customers' from the **Sample Tables** list of the Table Wizard dialogue box, to reveal a list of appropriate fields for that table, as shown above.

You can either select all the fields with the >> button, or you can select a few. For our example, we selected the following fields: CustomerID, CompanyName, BillingAddress, City, StateOrProvince, PostalCode, ContactTitle, PhoneNumber, FaxNumber and Notes, by highlighting each in turn and pressing the > button.

To change field names, highlight them in turn in the **Fields in my new table** list and click the **Rename Field** button to reveal the Rename field dialogue box shown here in Fig. 4.3.

Fig. 4.3 Renaming Fields

We suggest you change the selected field names to those listed below.

CompanyName	Name
BillingAddress	Address
City	Town
CustomerID	CustomerID
StateOrProvince	County
PostalCode	PostCode
ContactTitle	Contact
PhoneNumber	Phone
FaxNumber	Fax
Notes	Order

When you have completed renaming the field names, press the **Finish** button, which displays the Customers Table in Datasheet view ready for you to enter information, as shown in Fig. 4.4 below.

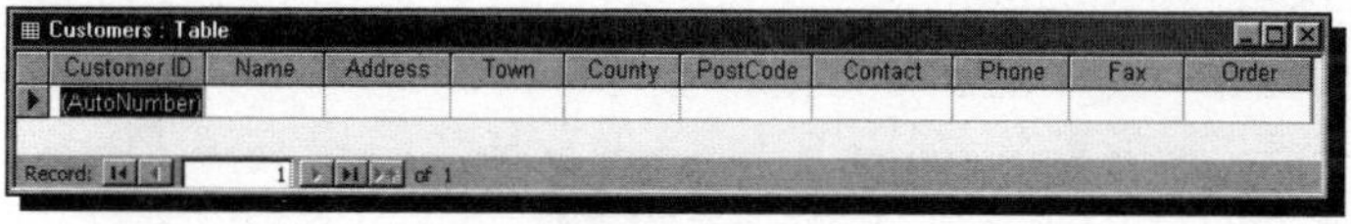

Fig. 4.4 The Empty Customers Table in Datasheet View

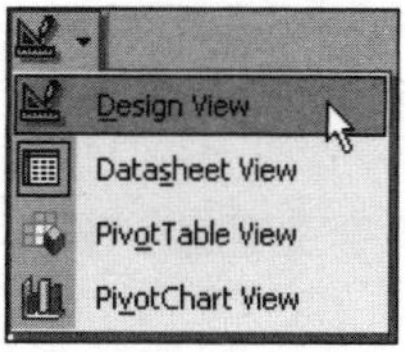

Fig. 4.5 The Design View Button Menu

From this view, to redesign the table, including changing its field names, click the **View** button shown here in Fig. 4.5, and choose the **Design View** option, or use the **View, Design View** main menu command. The table is then displayed in Design view, as shown in Fig. 4.6 on the next page.

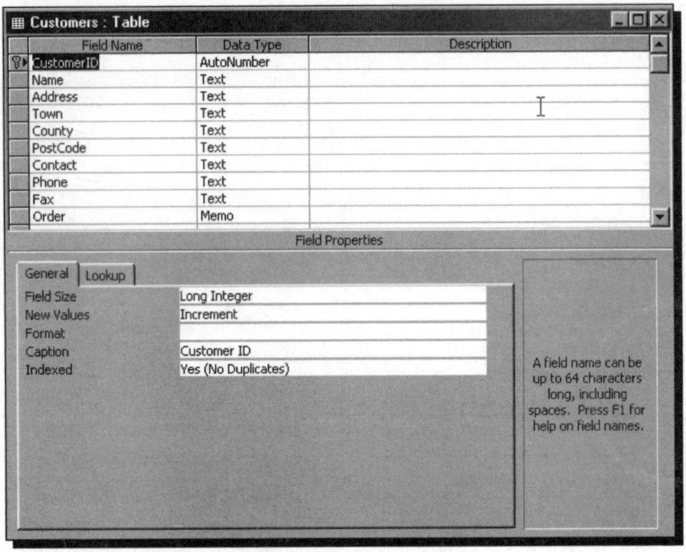

Fig. 4.6 The Empty Customers Table in Design View

In Design view you can change the data type and properties of the fields in the table and give each one a description which is then displayed when that field is used in the database.

As each field name is highlighted, a Field Properties box appears at the bottom of the screen. If you were using this Design view to rename fields, then you should also edit the name appearing against the Caption property, or remove it altogether.

Data Types

Next, click the cursor at the right end of the Data Type descriptor of the CustomerID field and click the down-arrow button which appears. This displays a drop-down list of data types, as shown here and explained on the next page.

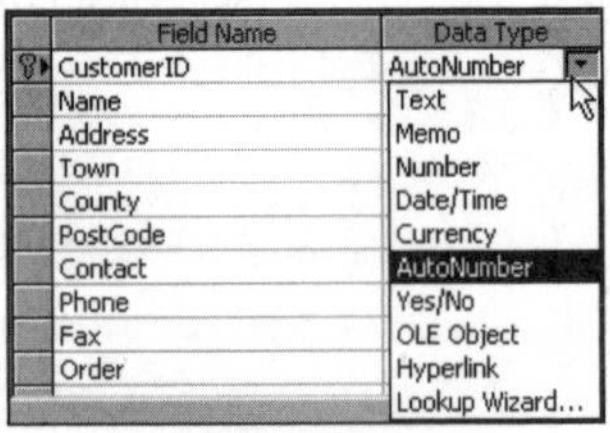

Fig. 4.7 List of Data Types

Data Type	Usage	Size
Text	Alphanumeric data	< 255 characters
Memo	Alphanumeric data, sentences and paragraphs	< 64,000 characters
Number	Numeric data	1, 2, 4, or 8 bytes (16 bytes for ReplicationID or Decimal)
Date/Time	Dates and times	8 bytes
Currency	Monetary values, stored with 4 decimal places of precision	8 bytes
AutoNumber	Unique value generated by Access for each new record	4 bytes (16 bytes for ReplicationID)
Yes/No	Boolean (true/false) data	<1 byte>
OLE Object	Pictures, graphs, or other ActiveX objects from other Windows-based applications	< about 1 gigabyte
Hyperlink	A link 'address' to a document or file on the Web, an intranet, or on a local area network.	< 2048 characters

As we intend to use the first four letters of a company's name as the CustomerID field in our database, change its current data type from Autonumber to Text. Then save the table by clicking the **Save** button, before changing the data type of the last field (Order) from Memo to AutoNumber.

Finally, place the cursor against the Phone and Fax fields and delete any entries against the Input Mask in the Field Properties box. If input masks are displayed here they will be for USA Phone and Fax numbers, and will not correspond to the entry form usually adopted in the UK, so they are best removed.

Click the Save icon again, or use the **File, Save** command to save your design changes, then click the **View** button (or use the **View, Datasheet View** command) to revert to the Customers table so that you can start entering the information below.

Customer ID	Name	Address	Town	County	Post Code	Contact
VORT	VORTEX Co. Ltd	Windy House	St. Austell	Cornwall	TR18 1FX	Brian Storm
AVON	AVON Construction	Riverside House	Stratford-on-Avon	Warwickshire	AV15 2QW	John Waters
BARR	BARROWS Associates	Barrows House	Bodmin	Cornwall	PL22 1XE	Mandy Brown
STON	STONEAGE Ltd	Data House	Salisbury	Wiltshire	SB44 1BN	Mike Irons
PARK	PARKWAY Gravel	Aggregate House	Bristol	Avon	BS55 2ZX	James Stone
WEST	WESTWOOD Ltd	Weight House	Plymouth	Devon	PL22 1AA	Mary Slim
GLOW	GLOWORM Ltd	Light House	Brighton	Sussex	BR87 4DD	Peter Summers
SILV	SILVERSMITH Co	Radiation House	Exeter	Devon	EX28 1PL	Adam Smith
WORM	WORMGLAZE Ltd	Glass House	Winchester	Hampshire	WN23 5TR	Richard Glazer
EALI	EALING Engines Design	Engine House	Taunton	Somerset	TN17 3RT	Trevor Miles
HIRE	HIRE Service Equipment	Network House	Bath	Avon	BA76 3WE	Nicole Webb
EURO	EUROBASE Co. Ltd	Control House	Penzance	Cornwall	TR15 8LK	Sarah Star

Fig. 4.8 Customers Table Data

The widths of the above fields were changed so that all fields could be visible on the screen at the same time. One way to do this is to place the cursor on the column separator until the cursor changes to the vertical split arrow, shown in Fig. 4.9, then drag this column separator to the right or left, to increase or decrease the width of the field.

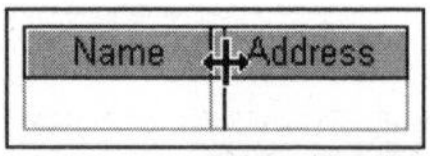

Fig. 4.9 Changing Column Width

For other methods of changing the widths of columns see the section later in this chapter.

Sorting a Database Table

As you enter information into a database table, you might elect to change the field headings by clicking the Design Table icon and editing a field name, say from Name to CompanyName. If you do this, when you return to the table in Datasheet view you will find that the records have sorted automatically in ascending order of the entries of the field in which you left the cursor while in Design view.

Contact	Phone	Fax	Order
Brian Storm	01776-223344	01776-224466	1
John Waters	01657-113355	01657-221133	2
Mandy Brown	01554-664422	01554-663311	3
Mike Irons	01765-234567	01765-232332	4
James Stone	01534-987654	01534-984567	5
Mary Slim	01234-667755	01234-669988	6
Peter Summers	01432-746523	01432-742266	7
Adam Smith	01336-997755	01336-996644	8
Richard Glazer	01123-654321	01123-651234	9
Trevor Miles	01336-010107	01336-010109	10
Nicole Webb	01875-558822	01875-552288	11
Sarah Star	01736-098765	01736-098567	12
			(AutoNumber)

Fig. 4.10 Remainder of Example Data

If you want to preserve the order in which you entered your data, then sort by the last field (Order) with its type as AutoNumber. This can be done at any time, even after you have finished entering all of the other information.

Sorting a database table in ascending order of an AutoNumber type field, results in the database table displaying in the order in which the data was originally entered in that table. In Fig 4.10 above, we show the Contact field, so that you can cross-check the original order of your Customer table, as well as the rest of the information in that table not shown in the screen dump of the previous page.

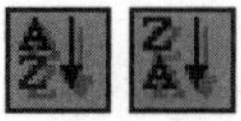

To sort a database table in ascending or descending order of the entries of any field, place the cursor in the required field and click either the **Sort Ascending** or **Sort Descending** button, shown here.

With the keyboard, select the **Records, Sort** command, then choose either the **Sort Ascending** or the **Sort Descending** option.

Applying a Filter to a Sort

If you would like to sort and display only records that fit selected criteria, use the **Records, Filter, Advanced Filter/Sort** command, which opens the Filter dialogue box, shown in Fig. 4.11 below.

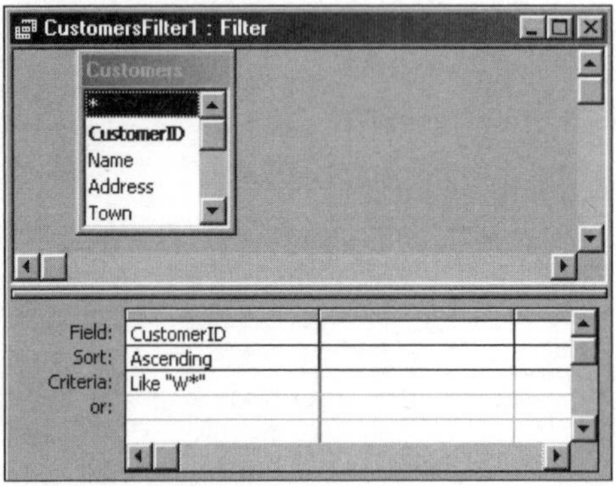

Fig. 4.11 Applying a Filter

The upper portion of the dialogue box displays all the fields in the Customers table, while the lower portion is where you enter your filter restrictions.

In our example here, we chose to view, in ascending order, the records within the CustomersID field that start with W - we typed W* and Access displayed *Like "W*"*.

When the **Apply Filter** button, shown here, is pressed the Customers table displays with only two entries, as can be seen in Fig. 4.12 below. To go back to the display of all the records, click the same icon again, which now appears depressed on the Toolbar, and has the name **Remove Filter**.

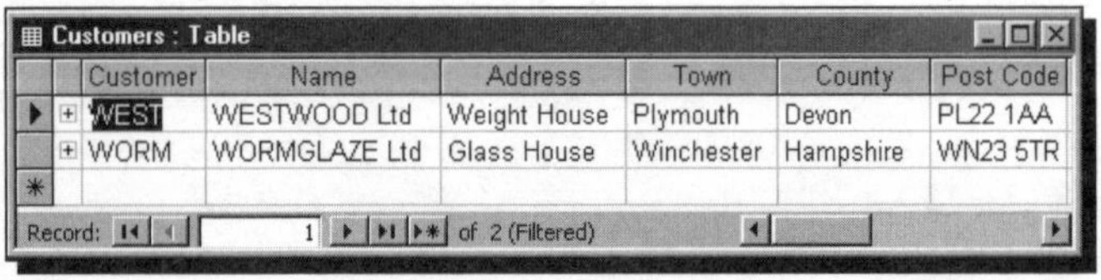

Customers : Table

Customer	Name	Address	Town	County	Post Code
WEST	WESTWOOD Ltd	Weight House	Plymouth	Devon	PL22 1AA
WORM	WORMGLAZE Ltd	Glass House	Winchester	Hampshire	WN23 5TR

Record: 1 of 2 (Filtered)

Fig. 4.12 The Result of Actioning the Filter

Note that both of these views of the table have a navigation bar at the bottom, so that you can easily find your way around the displayed records. When a filter is active the status displays as '(Filtered)', as shown above.

Using a Database Form

Once a table has been selected from the Database window,

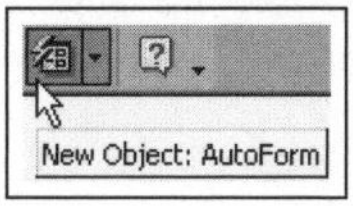

clicking the **New Object** toolbar button will automatically display each record of that table in form view. The created form for the Customers table is shown in Fig. 4.13 below.

Forms can be used to enter, change or view data. They are mainly used to improve the way data is displayed.

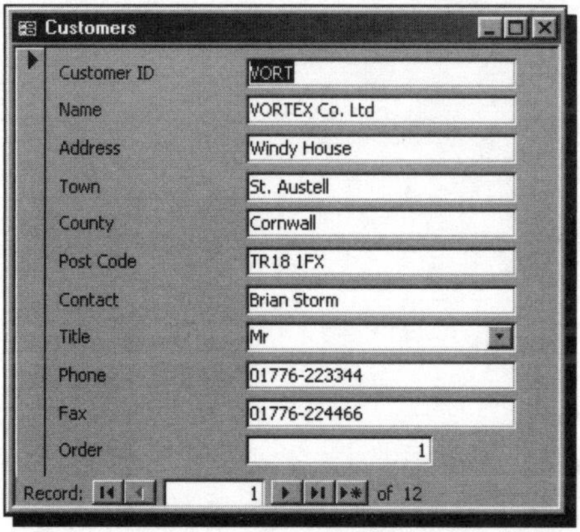

Fig. 4.13 The Automatically Created Customers Form

Forms can also be used to sort records in a database table in descending or ascending order of a selected field.

When you attempt to close a new **Form** window, you will be asked if you would like to save it. An Access database can have lots of different forms, each designed with a different purpose in mind. Saved forms are displayed in the Database window when you click the Forms object button. In the above example, we chose the default name suggested by Access, which was Customers.

In a later chapter we will discuss Forms and their design in some detail, including their customisation, but before we go any further we will now spend a little time looking at easy ways to manipulate the data in an Access database.

Selecting Data

As with most Windows programs, before you can carry out an action on part of a database, you must first select it. Selected data is highlighted as shown below.

Selecting Fields

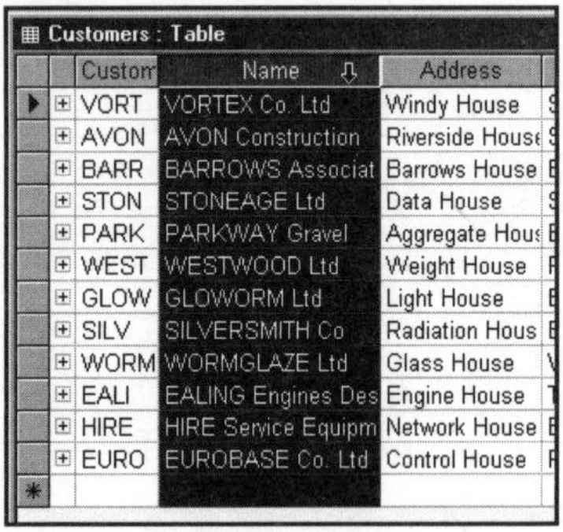

Fig. 4.14 Selecting a Table Field

A field is a vertical column in a database table. To select it, move the mouse over the field name at the top of the column, and when the pointer changes to a ⬇ shape, simply click to select the one field, or drag the pointer across several columns and release it to select those fields.

Selecting Records

A record, on the other hand, is a horizontal row in a database table. To select it, move the mouse into the area to the left of the record and when the pointer changes to a ➜ shape, simply click to select the one record, or drag the pointer up or down across several rows and release it to select those records.

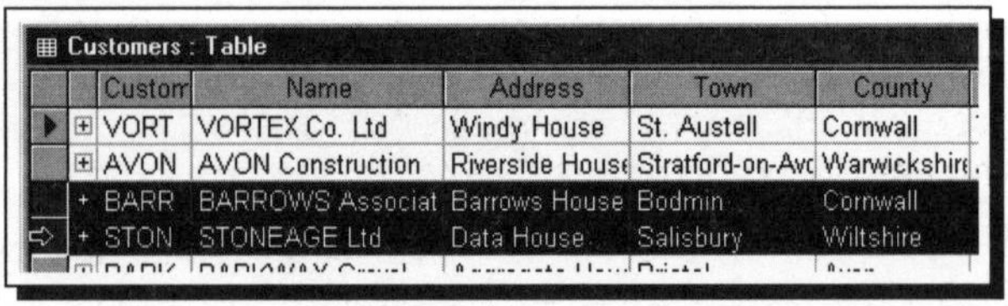

Fig. 4.15 Selecting Table Records

Selecting Cells

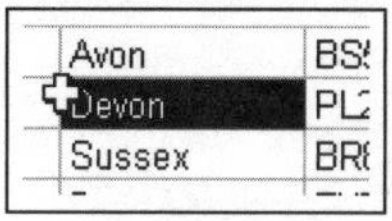

Fig. 4.16
Selecting a Cell

To select a cell, move the mouse over the left edge of the cell and the pointer will change to a ✥ shape. Simply click this pointer to select the cell, or drag it across the required cells and release it to select more than one.

Selecting Data in a Cell

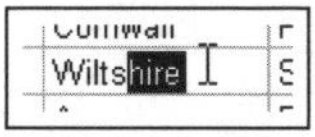

Fig. 4.17
Selecting Data

To select data actually inside a cell, position the I-beam pointer I in the data, left-click and drag the pointer to highlight the required data, as shown here in Fig. 4.17.

Zooming into a Cell

If you need to view or edit the contents of a cell that are not visible in a table because the column width is too narrow, you can open a zoom window on the cell. To do this, click the cell and press the <Shift+**F2**> key combination.

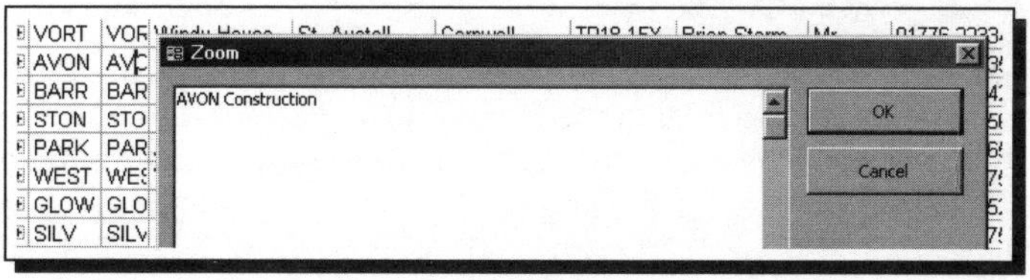

Fig. 4.18 Zooming in to the Contents of a Cell

Once the Zoom dialogue box opens, you can view the whole content of the cell. You can edit and change the font of the cell contents in this box as well, which makes life far easier as you can see what you are doing.

When you have finished with the cell, click the **OK** button to close the Zoom box. Any changes you made will be automatically saved for you.

Working with Data

Adding Records in a Table

Whether you are in Table view or Form view, to add a record, click the **New Record** button, shown here.

When in Table view, the cursor jumps to the first empty record in the table (the one with the asterisk in the box to the left of the first field). When in Form view, Access displays an empty form which can be used to add a new record.

Finding Records in a Table

In Table or Form view, to find a record click the **Find** toolbar button, use **Edit, Find**, or the <Ctrl+F> key combination. These all open the following Find and Replace dialogue box:

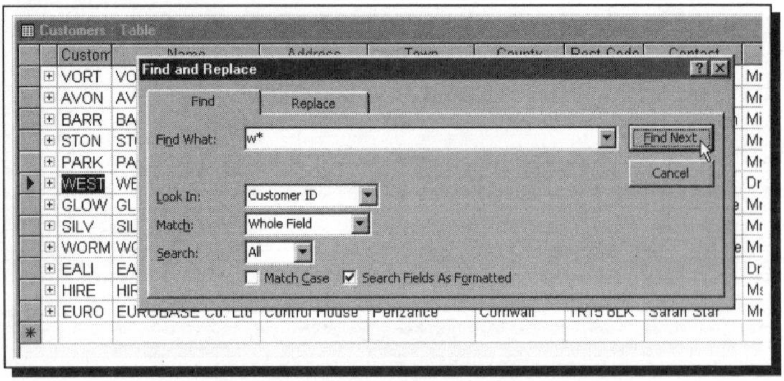

Fig. 4.19 Finding Matching Text in a Table

Note the field name in the **Look In** box, which is CustomerID, indicating that the cursor was in the CustomerID field before we actioned the Find command.

To find all the records starting with **w**, we typed **w*** in the **Find What** box. Pressing the **Find Next** button, highlights the first record with the CustomerID 'WEST', in our case.

Pressing the **Find Next** button again, highlights the next record that matches our select criteria.

Clicking the Replace tab opens the very powerful tool for replacing one text string for another, in individual fields, or whole tables or forms.

Deleting Records from a Table

To delete a record when in Table view, click in the box to the left of the record to highlight the entire record, then either click the **Delete Record** icon on the main toolbar, right-click and select **Delete Record**, as shown in Fig. 4.20 below, or press the <Del> key.

Fig. 4.20 Deleting a Record with the Shortcut Menu

To delete a record when in Form view, first display the record you want to delete, then click the **Delete Record** button on the main toolbar.

In both cases you will be given a warning and you will be asked to confirm your decision.

Fig. 4.21 The Delete Warning Box

As your database gets more complex you will link tables together and you will then find that Access won't let you delete any records that have related records in other tables.

The Office Clipboard

As is usual with Windows applications, the cutting and copying of objects and text places them on the clipboard. Microsoft Office XP comes with a new extra clipboard in which you can store up to 24 cut or copied items until they are needed. You can paste any of these stored items into Access or another Office application. Each item is displayed as a thumbnail on the new Clipboard Task Pane as shown in Fig. 4.22 below.

The Clipboard Task Pane

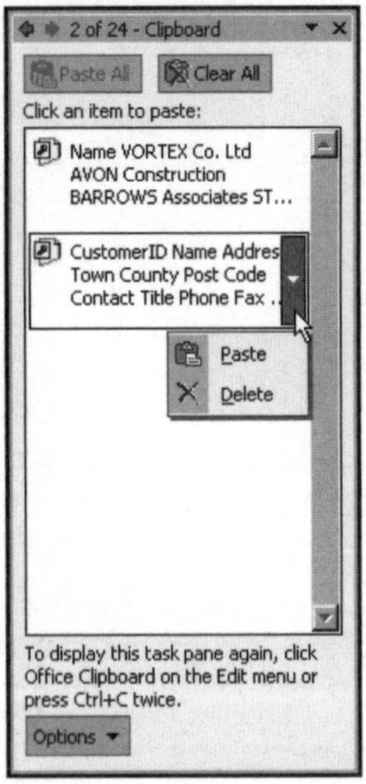

Fig. 4.22 The Clipboard Task Pane

If the Clipboard Task Pane does not open automatically you can open it with the **Edit**, **Office Clipboard** command, or by pressing the <Ctrl+C> keys twice. The latter method will only work if the **Show Office Clipboard Automatically** option has been selected in the task pane **Options** menu.

Fig. 4.22 shows the Clipboard holding two text items. The down arrow on the bottom item (with the selection square around it) has been clicked to open the **Paste** or **Delete** sub-menu. Clicking **Paste** will place the text current location in the database.

While the Clipboard Task Pane is active in any Office XP program, an icon like the one shown here is placed on the Windows task bar. This lets you easily access the pane, and also flags up how many items the clipboard contains.

Manipulating Table Columns

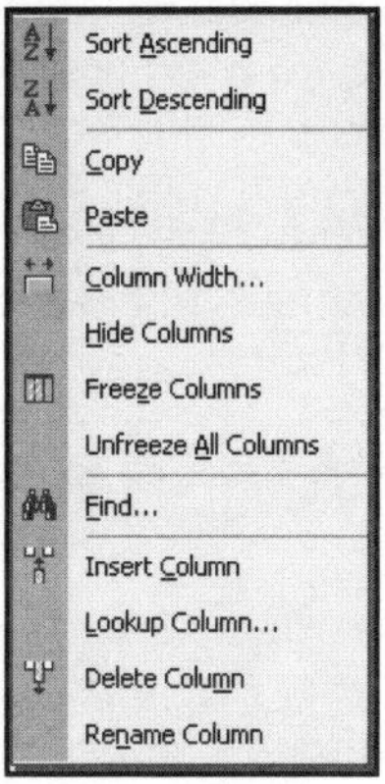

Fig. 4.23
Shortcut Menu

Perhaps the easiest way to manipulate the columns of an Access table is to select the column, or columns, and use the menu that is opened by right-clicking the column, as shown here in Fig. 4.23.

This gives a range of rapid options that are available. You can sort the column, or field, in ascending or descending order, **Copy** the column contents to the Office XP clipboard, and then **Paste** them to an empty column, either in the same table, or in another one.

The other menu features are described in the next few sections.

Adjusting Column Widths

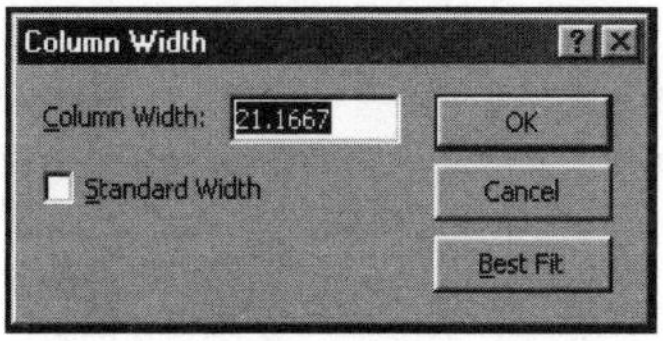

Fig. 4.24 Setting Column Widths

Selecting **Column Width** from the above menu opens the small box shown here, which gives you three options. You can type an exact width in the **Column Width** text box, select **Standard Width** to force the Access default width of about one 'screen inch', or click **Best Fit**. The last option sets the column width so that both the heading and all field values are visible. Not much use if you have long text items in your fields, but excellent for more simple columns.

On page 52 we saw that an easy, if imprecise, way to change the width of a column was to drag the ↔ shaped pointer in the column selector at the top of a column. There is also a quick way to select the 'Best Fit' width for a column, by double-clicking this ↔ pointer on the right border of the column selector.

Hiding Fields

To reduce the data displayed on the screen you may find it useful to hide one or more columns, by first selecting them and then using the **Hide Columns** command, from either the right-click shortcut menu, or the **Format** menu.

A hidden field is, of course, not deleted from the database, it is just made temporarily invisible. To unfreeze fields simply use the **Format**, **Unhide Columns** menu command.

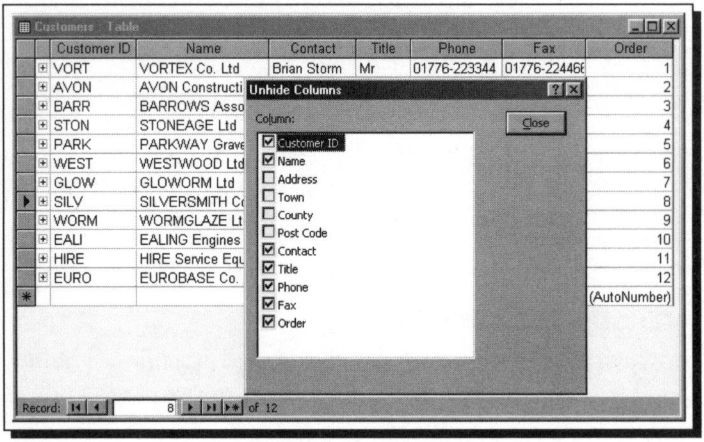

Fig. 4.25 Hiding and Unhiding Table Columns

This opens the dialogue box shown above. In this example we have hidden the four address fields, to unhide them we would need to check their boxes in the **Column** list and click **Close**.

Freezing Fields

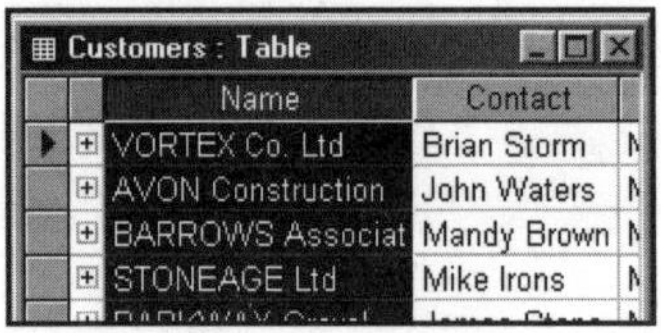

Fig. 4.26 A Frozen Column

The **Freeze Columns** menu option, from either the right-click shortcut menu, or the **Format** menu, moves selected columns to the left of a table and always displays them. In Fig. 4.26 the 'Name' field has been frozen.

You can only cancel this operation from the **Format** menu with the **Unfreeze All Columns** command. This, however, leaves the previously frozen columns still moved to the left of the table. As long as you have not saved the table with its columns frozen, you can close the table (without saving it) and re-open it in its original state. If you have saved the table, to return it to its original format you will have to move the fields back to where they 'started'.

Moving a Field

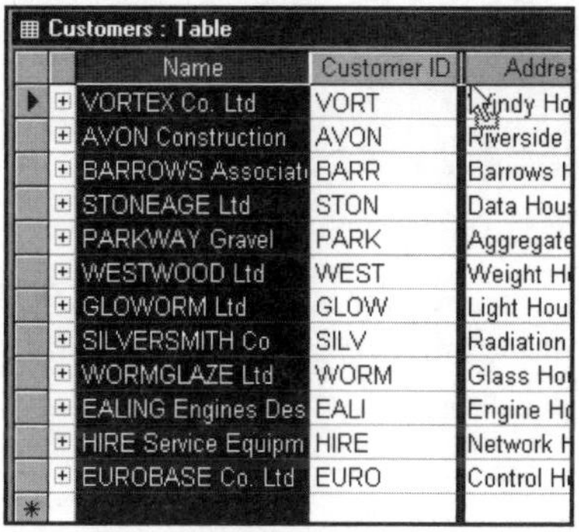

Customers : Table
Name
Customer ID
Addre
VORTEX Co. Ltd
VORT
AVON Construction
AVON
Riverside
BARROWS Associat
BARR
Barrows
STONEAGE Ltd
STON
Data Hou
PARKWAY Gravel
PARK
Aggregat
WESTWOOD Ltd
WEST
Weight H
GLOWORM Ltd
GLOW
Light Hou
SILVERSMITH Co
SILV
Radiation
WORMGLAZE Ltd
WORM
Glass Ho
EALING Engines Des
EALI
Engine H
HIRE Service Equipm
HIRE
Network
EUROBASE Co. Ltd
EURO
Control H

Fig. 4.27 Moving a Field

To move a field from its current position to a new position in a table, select the field you want to move, make sure it is not frozen, then click on the column selector so that the mouse pointer changes to that shown here, and drag the row to its new position.

Note that while you are dragging the field, a solid vertical bar shows where the field will be placed when the mouse button is released, as shown in Fig. 4.27 above.

Inserting, Renaming and Deleting Fields

To insert a field in a table, select and highlight the field to the right of where you want to insert the new field, right-click in it and select **Insert Column**, as shown in our composite in Fig. 4.28 on the next page. You could also use the **Insert, Column** main menu command.

Select your new column, which is named Field 1, and then use the **Rename Column** menu command, type the new name and press <Enter>. It's as easy as that.

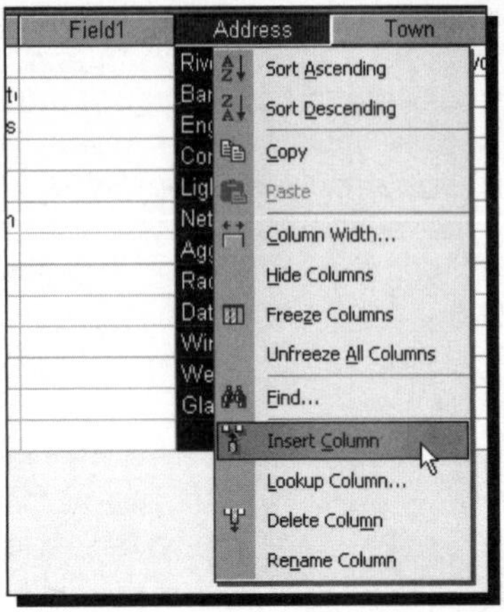

Fig. 4.28 Inserting a Column into a Table

To delete a field from a table, first select it, and then use the **Delete Column** shortcut menu command. You will be asked for confirmation before the column is actually deleted.

Adding a Lookup Column

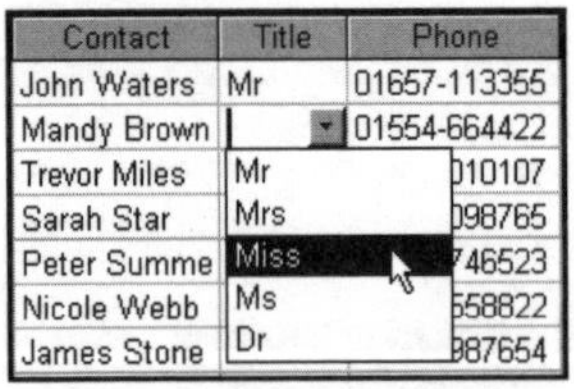

Fig. 4.29 A Lookup Column

There are times with most databases when a particular field requires only one of a limited number of possible entries. A good example might be the title field for the details of a person. These could be Mr, Mrs, Miss, Ms, Dr, etc. In Access you can include this list in a Lookup Column, as we show here in Fig 4.29.

When a cell is opened in this field a down-arrow button appears which, when clicked, opens the list of possibilities for you to choose from. Anything that saves time and typing when adding data has to be good news!

To open the Wizard to add such a column, select the column to the right of where you want it to be, right-click in it, and select **Lookup Column** from the shortcut menu.

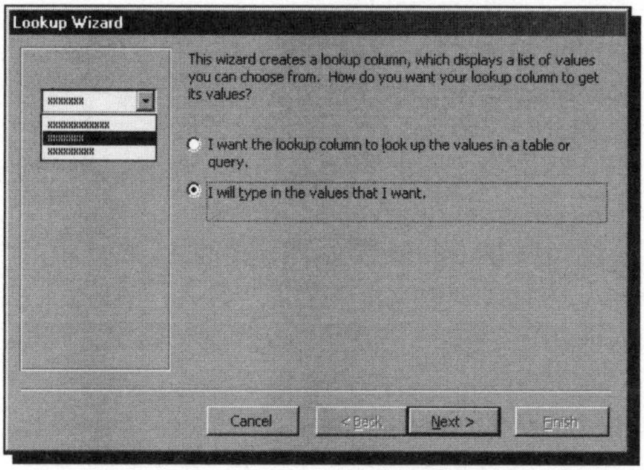

Fig. 4.30 The Lookup Wizard Opening Page

Opt to 'type in the values that I want' and click **Next** to go to the next Wizard box shown completed below.

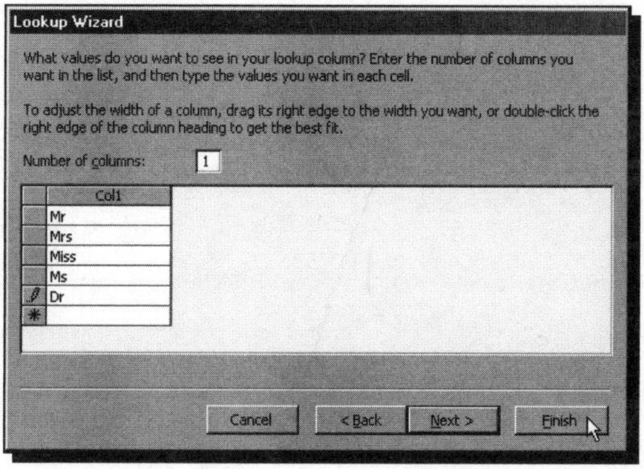

Fig. 4.31 Building a Lookup List

Make sure you select '1' as the **Number of columns** and then type the list entries one at a time. To move to the next cell press the <Tab> key. When you are happy with your list click the **Next** button and type in a suitable label for the field column. In our example 'Title' would be suitable, then click **Finish** to do just that.

Editing a Lookup List

If you need to make changes to a Lookup list in the future you can do it in the Design View of a database table.

In this view, click the field with the Lookup column and then select the **Lookup** tab, as shown on the next page. In the Row Source section of the Field Properties list you can see the values that will appear in the Lookup column.

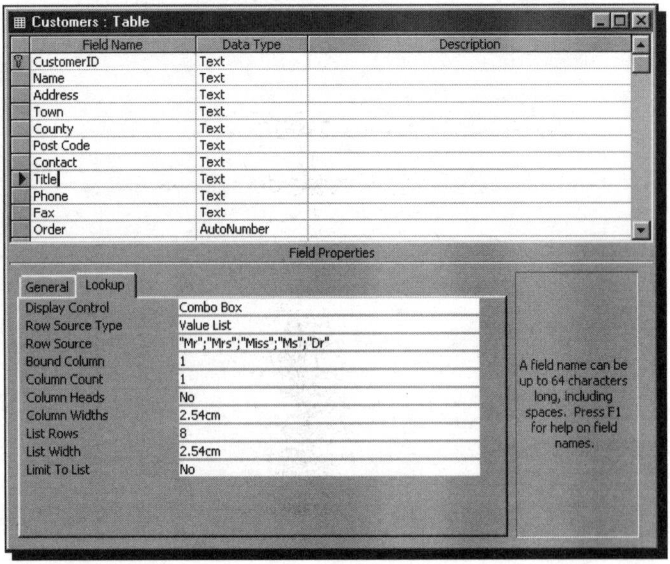

Fig. 4.32 Editing a Lookup List

You can edit this list as you wish, but make sure you keep its format intact. Items are included in inverted commas (“”) and separated with semicolons (;).

Printing a Table View

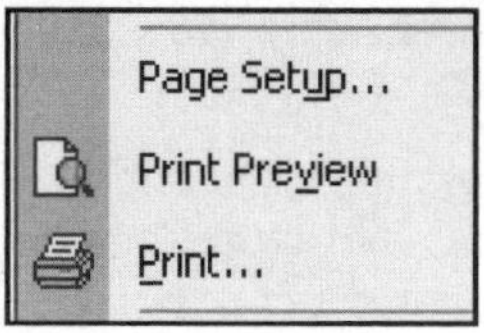

Fig. 4.33 Part of the File Menu

You can print a database table by clicking the **Print** icon, or by using the **File, Print** command to display the usual Windows Print dialogue box shown in Fig. 4.34 below. Alternatively, you can preview a database on screen with the **Print Preview** menu command, or toolbar icon, as shown in Fig 4.35 on the next page.

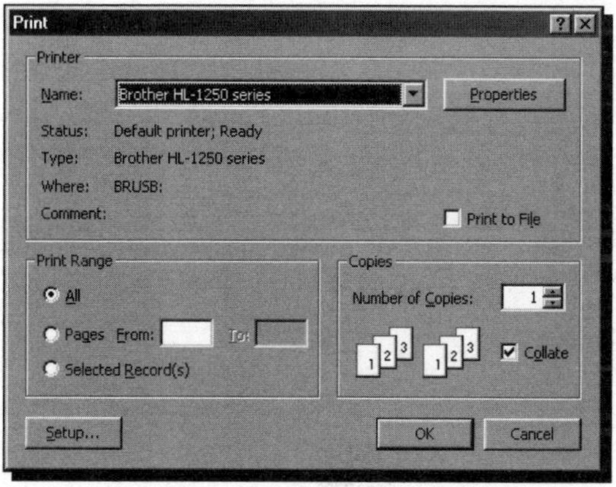

Fig. 4.34 The Windows Print Dialogue Box

However, printing directly from here, produces a predefined print-out, the format of which you cannot control, apart from the margins and print orientation. To control these, select the **Page Setup** menu option shown above.

For a better method of producing a printed output, see the Report Design section in a later chapter.

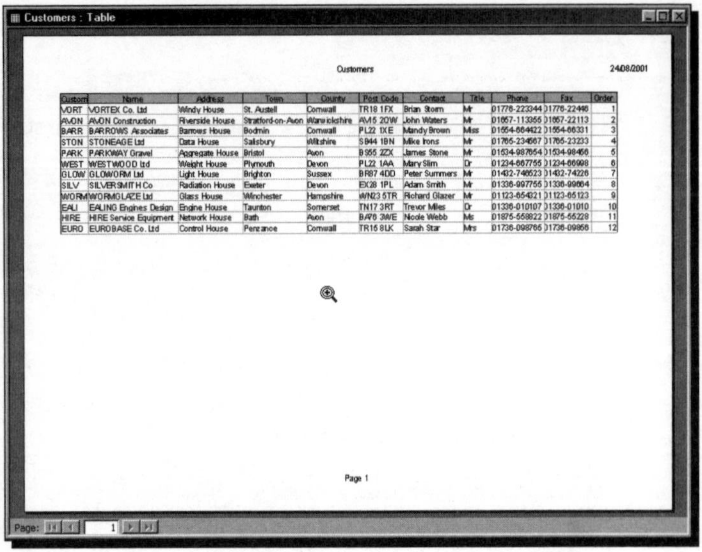
Customers : Table

Customers 24/08/2001

Custom	Name	Address	Town	County	Post Code	Contact	Title	Phone	Fax	Order
VORT	VORTEX Co. Ltd	Windy House	St. Austell	Cornwall	TR18 1FX	Brian Storm	Mr	01776-223344	01776-22446	1
AVON	AVON Construction	Riverside House	Stratford-on-Avon	Warwickshire	AV15 2QW	John Waters	Mr	01657-113355	01657-22113	2
BARR	BARROWS Associates	Barrows House	Bodmin	Cornwall	PL22 1XE	Mandy Brown	Miss	01554-664422	01554-66331	3
STON	STONEAGE Ltd	Data House	Salisbury	Wiltshire	SB44 1BN	Mike Irons	Mr	01765-234567	01765-23233	4
PARK	PARKWAY Gravel	Aggregate House	Bristol	Avon	BS55 2ZX	James Stone	Mr	01534-987654	01534-98456	5
WEST	WESTWOOD Ltd	Weight House	Plymouth	Devon	PL22 1AA	Mary Slim	Dr	01234-667755	01234-66998	6
GLOW	GLOWORM Ltd	Light House	Brighton	Sussex	BR87 4DD	Peter Summers	Mr	01432-746523	01432-74226	7
SILV	SILVERSMITH Co	Radiation House	Exeter	Devon	EX28 1PL	Adam Smith	Mr	01336-997755	01336-99664	8
WORM	WORMGLAZE Ltd	Glass House	Winchester	Hampshire	WN23 5TR	Richard Glazer	Mr	01123-654321	01123-65123	9
EALI	EALING Engines Design	Engine House	Taunton	Somerset	TN17 3RT	Trevor Miles	Dr	01336-010107	01336-01010	10
HIRE	HIRE Service Equipment	Network House	Bath	Avon	BA76 3WE	Nicole Webb	Ms	01875-558822	01875-55228	11
EURO	EUROBASE Co. Ltd	Control House	Penzance	Cornwall	TR16 8LK	Sarah Star	Mrs	01736-098765	01736-09856	12

Page 1

Page: 1

Fig. 4.35 A Print Preview of the Customers Table

5

Relational Database Design

In order to be able to discuss relational databases, we will add an Orders table to the database of the previous chapter. To do this go through the following steps.

- Open the **Adept 1** database, select **Tables** from the **Objects** list in the Database window and use the **New** button to add an Orders table to it.
- Select **Table Wizard** from the New Table box and select Orders from the displayed **Sample Tables** list. Next, select the five fields displayed in Fig. 5.1 below under **Fields in my new table** from the **Sample Fields** list, and press the **Next** button.

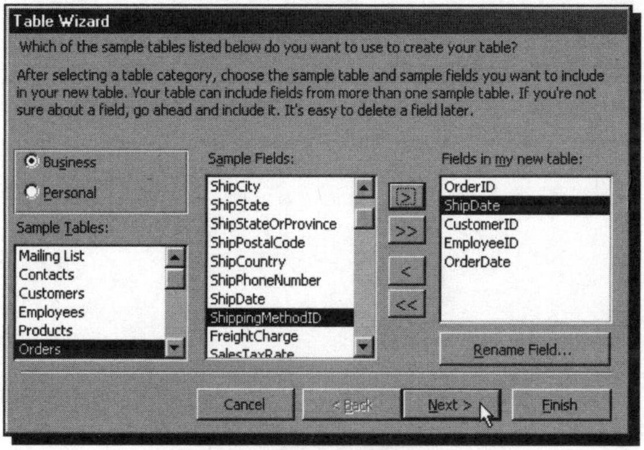

Fig. 5.1 The Table Wizard

This displays the dialogue box shown in Fig. 5.2, in which you can, if you want, change the name of the table. We elected to accept the default name, but we clicked the **No, I'll set the primary key** radio button before pressing the **Next** key.

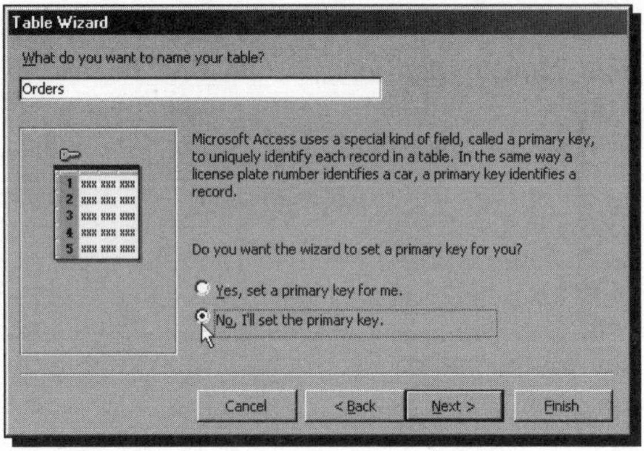

Fig. 5.2 Box 2 of the Table Wizard

* In the next dialogue box (Fig. 5.3) you can select which field will hold data that is unique for each record. The key field must be unique in a table, and the OrderID field satisfies this requirement. This field is used by Access for fast searches.

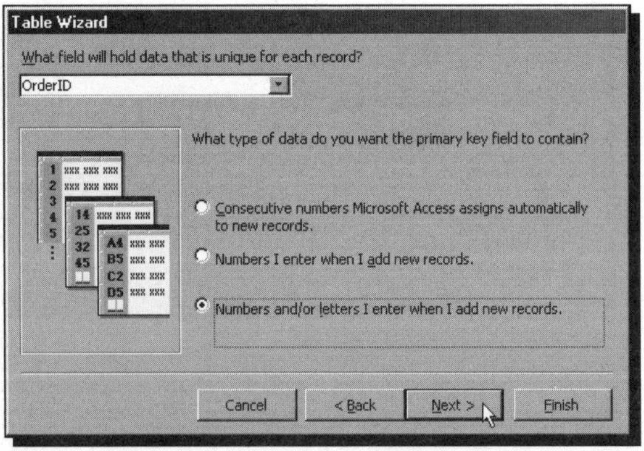

Fig. 5.3 Box 3 of the Table Wizard

* Click the **Numbers and/or letters I enter when I add new records** radio button, before you press the **Next** button again.

In the next dialogue box, shown in Fig. 5.4, you specify whether the new table is related to any other tables in the database. The default is 'not related'.

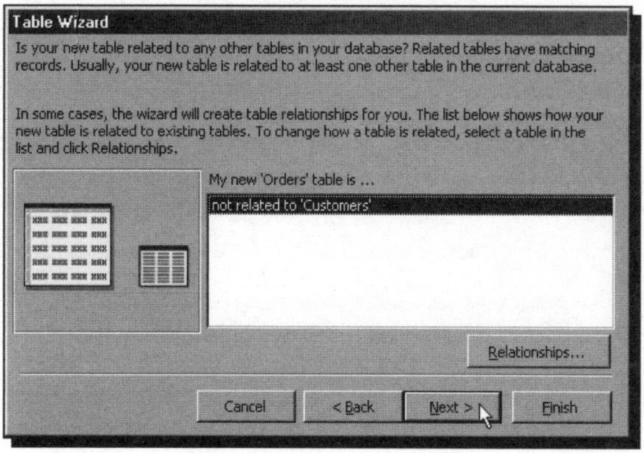

Fig. 5.4 Box 4 of the Table Wizard

- Accept the default option, and press the **<u>N</u>ext** button to reveal the final dialogue box, shown in Fig. 5.5.

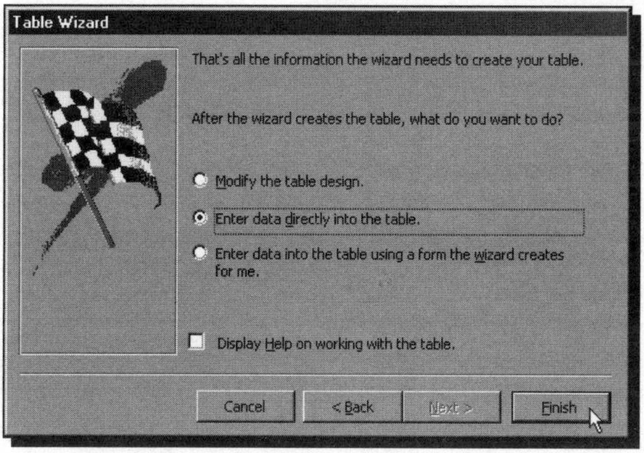

Fig. 5.5 The Final Box of the Table Wizard

- Select the second option and press the **<u>F</u>inish** button, to let the Wizard create your table.

Although the two tables are actually related, we chose at this stage to tell the Wizard that they are not. This might appear to you as odd, but the Wizard makes certain assumptions about unique fields (for example, that ID fields are numbers), which is not what we want. We chose to remain in control of the design of our database and, therefore, we will define the relationship between the two tables later.

The Wizard displays the newly created table ready for you to enter your data. However, before doing so, use the Design Table facility, as discussed previously, to change the Data Types of the selected Field Names to those displayed below.

Orders : Table

Field Name	Data Type	Description
OrderID	Text	
CustomerID	Text	
EmployeeID	Text	
OrderDate	Date/Time	
ShipDate	Date/Time	

Fig. 5.6 The Data Types of the Orders Table

The information, or data, you need to enter in the Orders table is shown in Fig. 5.7 below.

Orders : Table

Order ID	Customer ID	Employee ID	Order Date	Ship Date
97002STO	STON	C.H. Wills	20/02/2001	25/04/2001
97006PAR	PARK	A.D. Smith	13/03/2001	16/04/2001
97010WES	WEST	W.A. Brown	15/03/2001	26/04/2001
97018GLO	GLOW	L.S. Stevens	25/04/2001	19/05/2001
97025SIL	SILV	S.F. Adams	28/04/2001	22/05/2001
97029WOR	WORM	C.H. Wills	20/05/2001	13/06/2001
97039EAL	EALI	A.D. Smith	30/05/2001	25/06/2001
97045HIR	HIRE	W.A. Brown	18/06/2001	08/07/2001
97051EUR	EURO	L.S. Stevens	25/06/2001	19/07/2001
97064AVO	AVON	S.F. Adams	20/07/2001	15/08/2001
97085VOR	VORT	A.D. Smith	20/01/2001	10/02/2001
97097AVO	AVON	W.A. Brown	25/01/2001	14/02/2001
97099BAR	BARR	S.F. Adams	01/02/2001	02/03/2001

Record: 1 of 13

Fig. 5.7 Sample data for the Orders Table

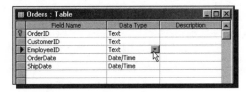

Relationships

Information held in two or more tables of a database is normally related in some way. In our case, the two tables, Customers and Orders, are related by the CustomerID field.

To build up relationships between tables, press the **Relationships** button on the main Access Toolbar, shown here. This opens the following window in which the index field in each table is emboldened.

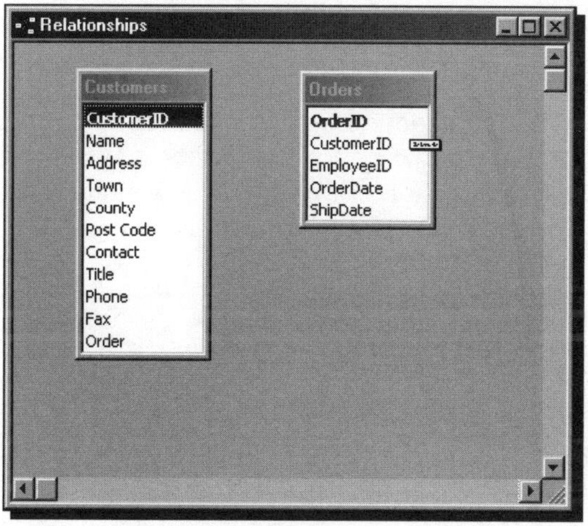

Fig. 5.8 The Relationships Window

You can build relationships between tables by dragging a field name from one table into another. In Fig. 5.8 above, we have dragged CustomerID from the Customers table to the required field in the other table, in this case CustomerID in the Orders table. Releasing the mouse button opens the dialogue box shown in Fig. 5.9.

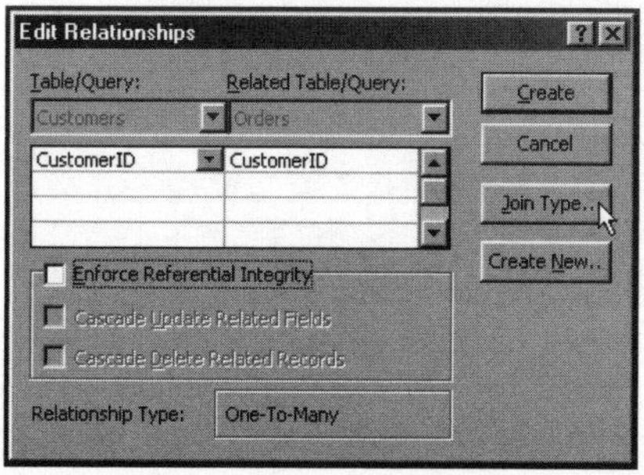

Fig. 5.9 Editing Relationships

Pressing the **Join Type** button on this Edit Relationships dialogue box opened yet another box (Fig. 5.10).

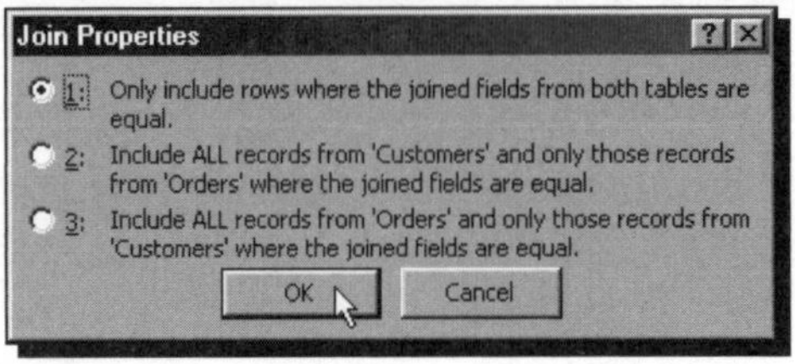

Fig. 5.10 Setting the Join Properties

In this Join Properties dialogue box you can specify the type of join Access should create in new queries - more about this later. For the present, press the OK button on the Join Properties dialogue box, to close it, then check the **Enforce Referential Integrity** box in the Edit Relationships dialogue box, and press the **Create** button.

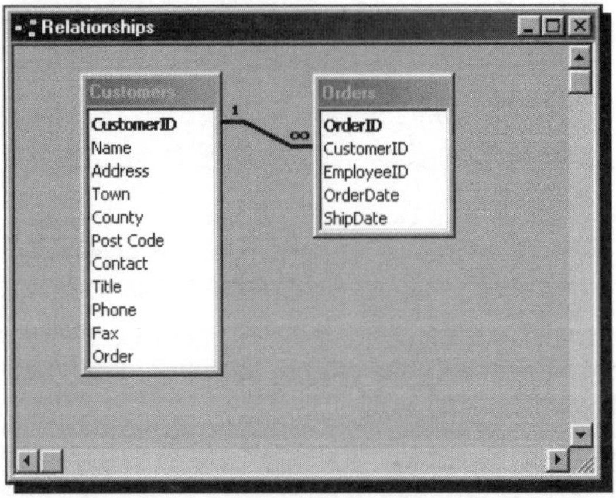

Fig. 5.11 The Completed Table Relationship

Access creates and graphically displays the chosen type of relationship in the Relationships window shown here in Fig. 5.11. Note the relationship '1 customer to many (∞) orders' symbolism in the Relationships window. Before leaving the Relationships window Access will ask if you want to save your changes, which you probably do.

Because Access is a relational database, data can be used in queries from more than one table at a time. As we have seen, if the database contains tables with related data, the relationships can be defined easily.

Usually, the matching fields have the same name, as in our example of Customers and Orders tables. In the Customers table, the CustomerID field is the primary field and relates to the CustomerID field in the Orders table - there can be several orders in the Orders table from one customer in the Customers table.

The various types of relationships are as follows:

- Inherited - for attaching tables from another Access database. The original relationships of the attached database can be used in the current database.

- Referential - for enforcing relationships between records according to certain rules, when you add or delete records in related tables belonging to the same database. For example, you can only add records to a related table, if a matching record already exists in the primary table, and you cannot delete a record from the primary table if matching records exist in a related table.

Viewing and Editing Relationships

At any time you can view the current relationships between tables, by clicking the Relationships icon and opening the Relationships dialogue box.

To edit a relationship, double-click the left mouse button on the inclined line joining the two tables. If you have difficulty with this action, first point to the relationship line and click once to embolden it, then use the **Relationships**, **Edit Relationship** command. Either of these two actions will open the Edit Relationships dialogue box in which you can change the various options already discussed.

A given relationship can easily be removed altogether by first activating it (pointing and clicking to embolden it), then

pressing the **Clear Layout** toolbar button. A confirmation dialogue box will be displayed, as shown in Fig. 5.12 below.

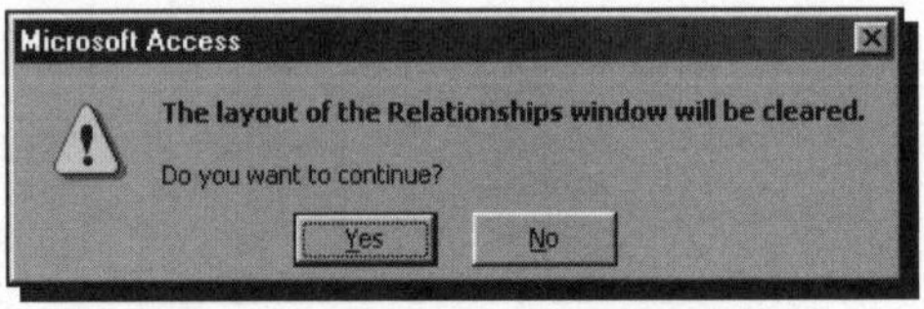

Fig. 5.12 The Last Chance to Change Your Mind!

To delete a table, you must first detach it from other tables, then select it in the Database window and press the **Delete** button. Think before you do this!

If you are into using right-click shortcut menus, and hopefully you are by now, the above actions can be much more easily carried out this way!

Creating an Additional Table

As an exercise, create a third table using the Table Wizard and select Invoices from the displayed **Sample Tables** list. Next, select the five fields displayed below in Design View - the names and their data types have been changed as shown in Fig. 5.13.

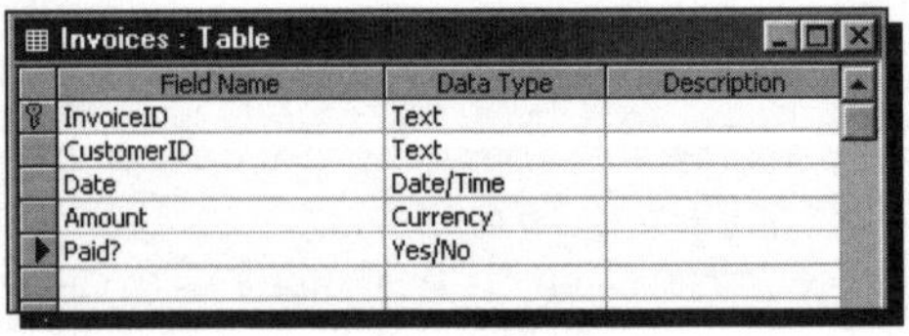

Invoices : Table

Field Name	Data Type	Description
InvoiceID	Text	
CustomerID	Text	
Date	Date/Time	
Amount	Currency	
Paid?	Yes/No	

Fig. 5.13 Field Names and Data Types for the Invoices Table

Next, enter the data given in Fig. 5.14 on the next page and build up appropriate relationships between the Invoices table, the Customers table and the Orders table, as shown in Fig 5.15, also on the next page.

Invoices : Table

Invoice No	Customer ID	Date	Amount	Paid?
AD9701	VORT	25/04/2001	£120.84	No
AD9702	AVON	16/04/2001	£103.52	Yes
AD9703	BARR	26/04/2001	£99.32	No
AD9704	STON	19/05/2001	£55.98	No
AD9705	PARK	22/05/2001	£180.22	No
AD9706	WEST	13/06/2001	£68.52	No
AD9707	GLOW	25/06/2001	£111.56	No
AD9708	SILV	08/07/2001	£123.45	Yes
AD9709	WORM	19/07/2001	£35.87	No
AD9710	EALI	15/08/2001	£58.95	No
AD9711	HIRE	10/02/2001	£290.00	No
AD9712	EURO	14/02/2001	£150.00	No
AD9713	AVON	02/03/2001	£135.00	No

Record: 13 of 13

Fig. 5.14 Sample Data for the Invoices Table

The relationships between the three tables should be arranged as shown in Fig. 5.15 below.

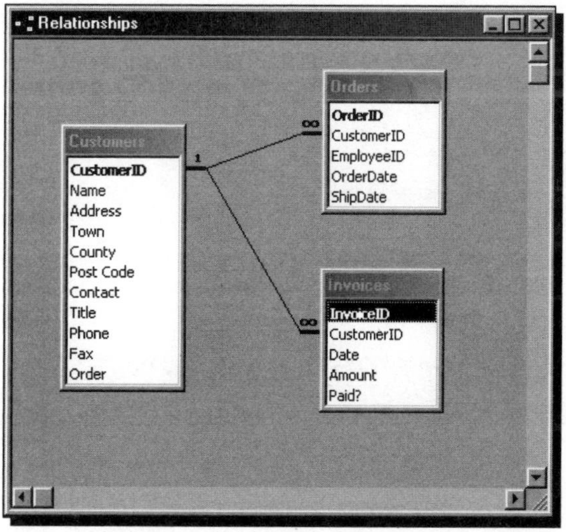

Fig. 5.15 The Final Table Relationships

Once the relationships between tables have been established, you can create queries, forms, and reports to display information from several tables at once.

It is important that you should complete this exercise, as it consolidates what we have done so far and we will be using all three tables in what comes next. So go ahead and try it.

Help on Relationships

If you need more help coming to terms with database relationships there is a lot of detail in the Access Help facility, as shown in Fig. 5.16 below. A good place to start would be the section *About relationships in an Access database.*

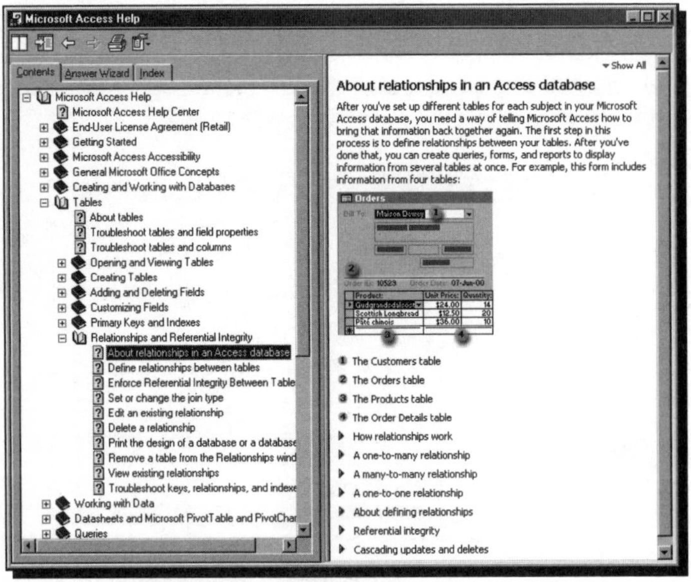

Fig. 5.16 The Access Help System on Relationships

6

Creating Queries

In Access you create a query so that you can ask questions about the data in your database tables. For example, we could find out whether we have more than one order from the same customer in our Adept database.

To do this, start Access, load the **Adept 1** database, and in the Database window click the Queries button in the **Objects** column, followed by the **New** button which opens the New Query dialogue box shown in Fig. 6.1 below.

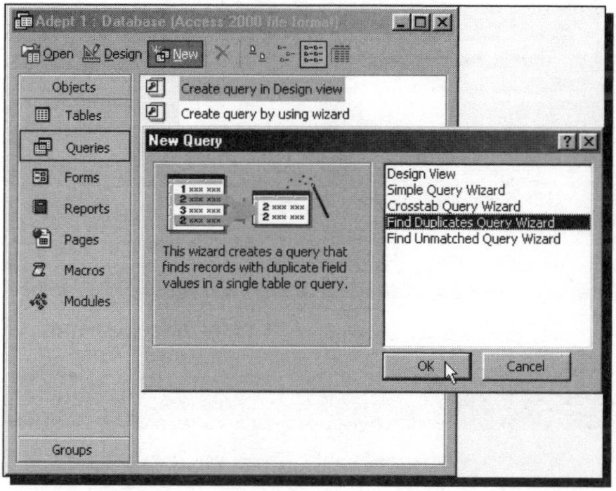

Fig. 6.1 Creating a Query in Access

Selecting **Find Duplicates Query Wizard**, as shown here, and clicking **OK** opens the first of the Find Duplicates Query Wizard dialogue boxes which are all displayed in the series of screen-dumps on the next page.

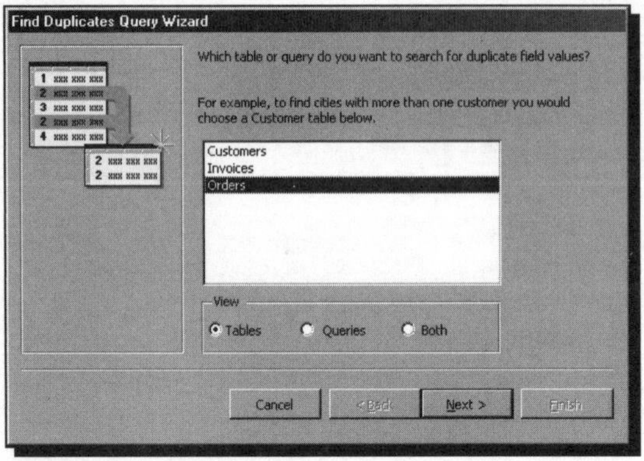

Fig. 6.2

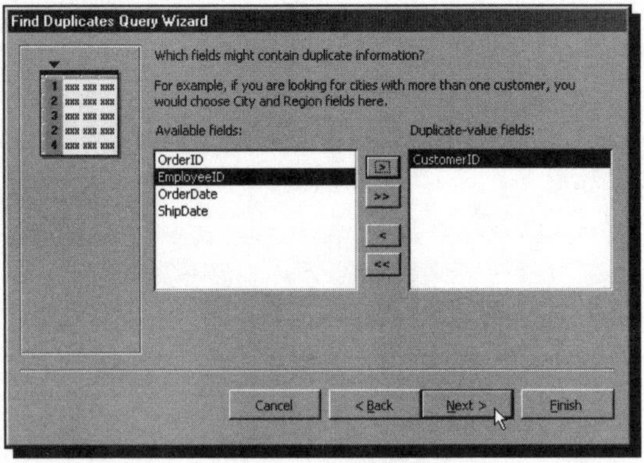

Fig. 6.3

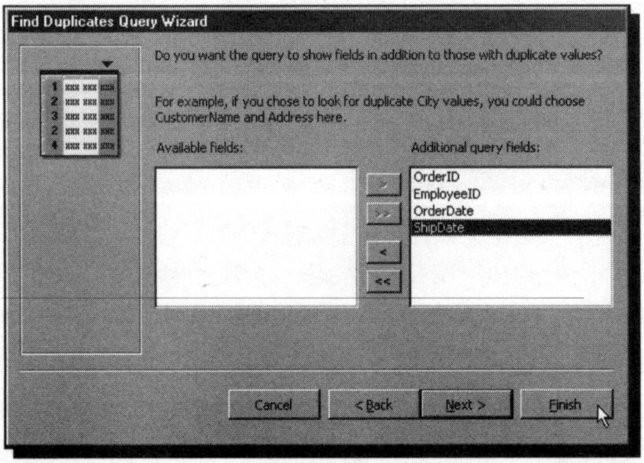

Fig. 6.4

In the first box (Fig. 6.2) select the Orders table from the displayed database tables and press the **Next** button.

In the next dialogue box (Fig. 6.3) select **CustomerID** as the field you want to check for duplicate values, then press the > button, followed by the **Next** button.

Finally, select the additional fields you would like to see along with the duplicate values, by selecting those you want from the last dialogue box (Fig. 6.4), either one at a time or, if you decide to select all of them, as shown here, by clicking the >> button. Clicking the **Finish** button then displays the Select Query results window shown in Fig. 6.5 below.

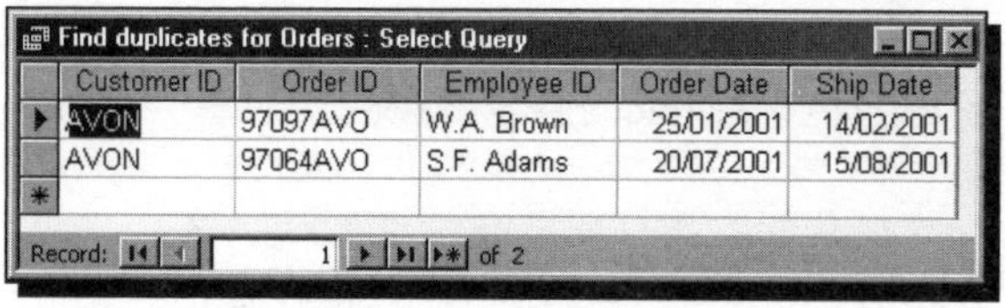

Fig. 6.5 The Select Query Results

If you examine the original Orders table, you will indeed find that it contains two orders from AVON. When you close this window, by clicking its X close button, you will find the new entry 'Find duplicates for Orders' has been added to the Queries list in the Database window, as shown in Fig. 6.6 below.

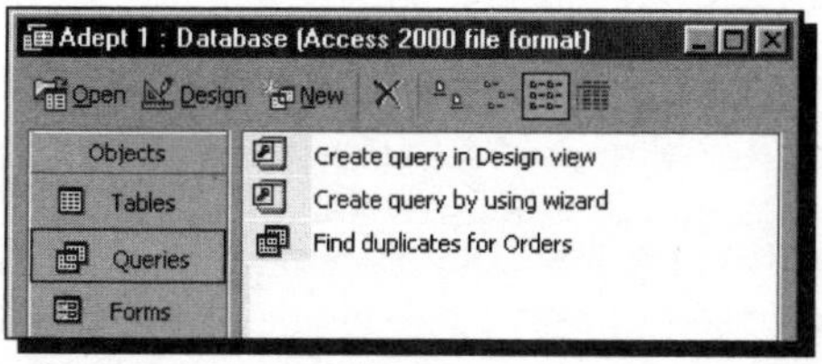

Fig. 6.6 The New Query Added to the Database Window

Once a query has been set up in Access you can action it at any time by double-clicking its name in the Database Window.

Types of Queries

The query we have created so far, is known as a *Select Query*, which is the most common type of query. However, with Access you can also create and use other types of queries, as follows:

- **Crosstab query** - used to present data with row and column headings, just like a spreadsheet. These can be used to summarise large amounts of data in a more readable form.
- **Action queries** - used to make changes to many records in one operation. They can consist of make-table, delete, update and append queries. For example, you might like to remove from a given table all records that meet certain criteria. Obviously, this type of query has to be treated with care!
- **Union query** - used to match fields from two or more tables.
- **Pass-through query** - used to pass commands to a SQL (pronounced 'sequel') database (see below).
- **Data-definition query** - used to create, change, or delete tables in an Access database using SQL statements.
- **Subquery** - consists of an SQL SELECT statement inside another select query or action query.

SQL stands for Structured Query Language, often used to query, update, and manage relational databases. Each query created by Access has an associated SQL statement that defines the action of that query. Thus, if you are familiar with SQL, you can use such statements to view and modify queries, or set form and report properties. However, these actions can be done more easily with the QBE (query-by-example) grid, to be discussed next. If you design union queries, pass-through queries, or data-definition queries, then you must use SQL statements, as these types of queries can not be designed with the QBE grid.

Finally, to create a sub-query, you use the QBE grid, but you enter a SQL SELECT statement for criteria, as we shall see in the next QBE grid example.

The Query Window

The Query window is a graphical query-by-example (QBE) tool. Because of Access' graphical features, you can use the mouse to select, drag, and manipulate objects in the query window to define how you would like to see your data.

An example of a ready-made Query window can be seen by selecting the Find duplicates for Orders query and clicking the **Design** button on the Database window. This action opens the Select Query design window shown below.

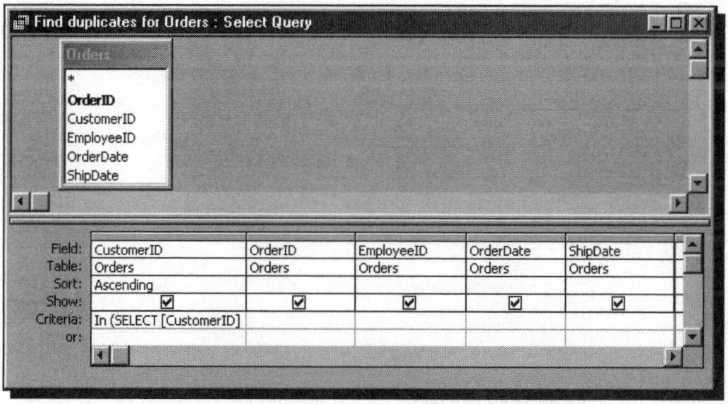

Fig. 6.7 The Select Query Design Window

You can add a table to the top half of the Query window by simply dragging it from the Database window. To remove it again, simply right-click in it and select **Remove Table** from the shortcut menu. Similarly, you can add fields to the bottom half of the Query window (the QBE grid) by dragging fields from the tables on the top half of the Query window. In addition, the QBE grid is used to select the sort order of the data, or insert criteria, such as SQL statements.

To see the full SQL SELECT statement written by Access as the criteria selection when we first defined the query, use the **View, SQL View** command.

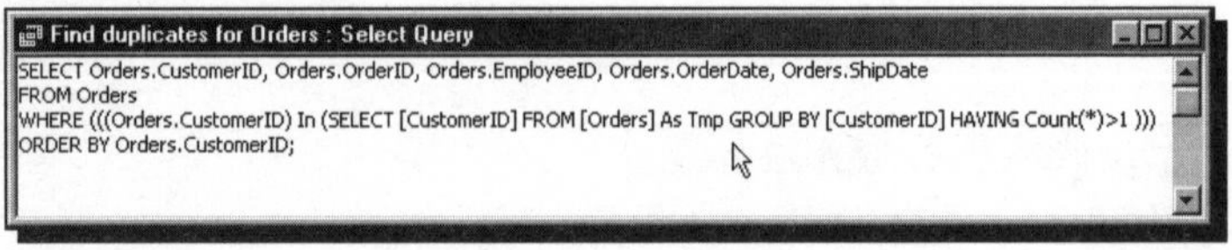

Fig. 6.8 The Example Query Written in SQL

Note the part of the statement which states 'As Tmp GROUP' pointed to above. Access collects the data you want as a temporary group, called a *dynaset*. This special set of data behaves like a table, but it is not a table; it is a dynamic view of the data from one or more tables, selected and sorted by the particular query.

Creating a New Query

Another way to create a new query is in the Design view. In the Database window, first click the Queries button in the **Objects** list and then double-click the option **Create query in Design view**, as shown in Fig. 6.9 below. This opens both the Select Query and the Show Table dialogue boxes shown in Fig. 6.10 on the next page.

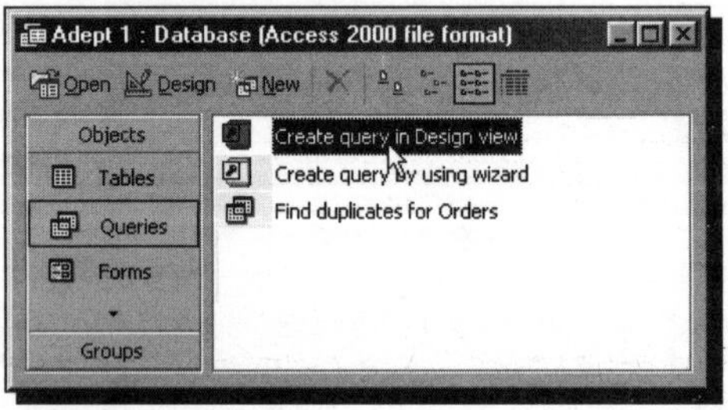

Fig. 6.9 Creating a New Query in Design View

In our example, the Invoices and Customers tables were then added to the Select Query window, by selecting each in the Show Table box and clicking the **Add** button. The Show Table box was then closed by clicking the **Add** button.

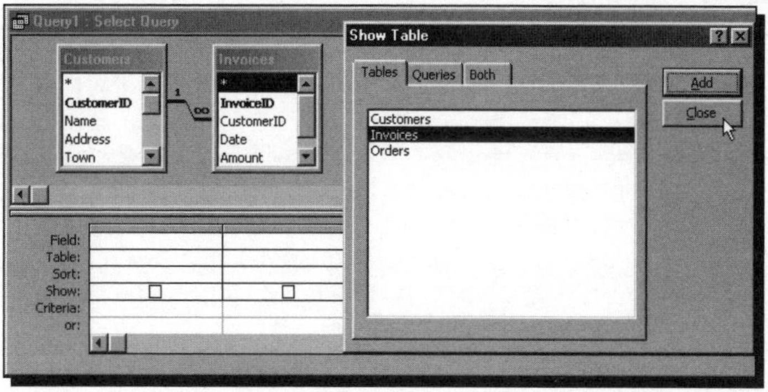

Fig. 6.10 Adding Tables from the Show Table Box

Adding Fields to a Query Window

In Fig. 6.11 below we show a screen in which the Paid?, InvoiceID and Amount fields have been dragged from the Invoices table and added to the Query window. In addition, the Name and Contact fields have been dragged from the Customers table and placed on the Query window, while the Phone field from the Customers table is about to be added to the Query window.

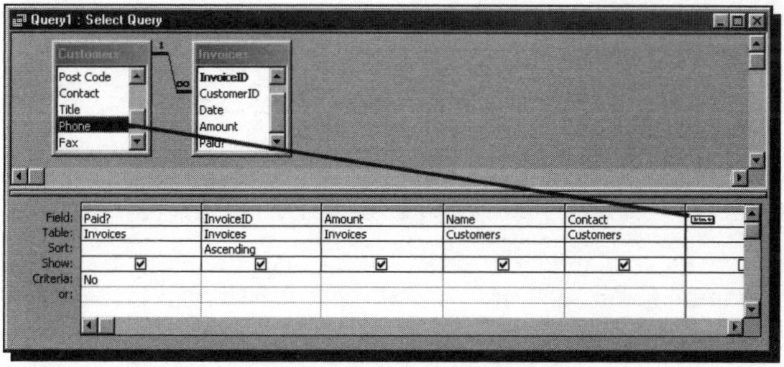

Fig. 6.11 Building a Query Manually

Having dragged these six fields from the two tables onto the QBE grid, we have added the word 'No' as the criteria on the Paid? field and selected Ascending as the Sort for the InvoiceID field, as shown above.

Note that the Invoices and Customers tables are joined by a line that connects the two CustomerID fields. This join line was created when we designed the tables and their relationships in the previous chapter. Even if you have not created these relationships, Access will join the tables in a query automatically when the tables are added to a query, provided each table has a field with the same name and a compatible data type and one of those fields is a primary key. A primary field is displayed in bold in the Query window.

If you have not created relationships between your tables yourself, or Access has not joined your tables automatically, you can still use related data in your query by joining the tables in the Query window.

Clicking the **Run** button on the toolbar, shown here, instantly displays all the unpaid invoices with the details you have asked for, as follows:

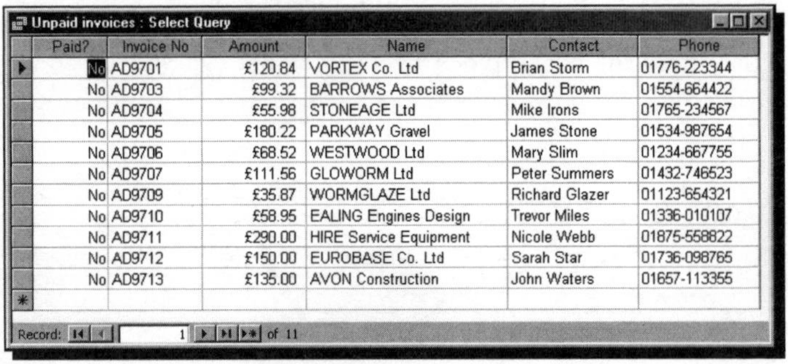

Paid?	Invoice No	Amount	Name	Contact	Phone
No	AD9701	£120.84	VORTEX Co. Ltd	Brian Storm	01776-223344
No	AD9703	£99.32	BARROWS Associates	Mandy Brown	01554-664422
No	AD9704	£55.98	STONEAGE Ltd	Mike Irons	01765-234567
No	AD9705	£180.22	PARKWAY Gravel	James Stone	01534-987654
No	AD9706	£68.52	WESTWOOD Ltd	Mary Slim	01234-667755
No	AD9707	£111.56	GLOWORM Ltd	Peter Summers	01432-746523
No	AD9709	£35.87	WORMGLAZE Ltd	Richard Glazer	01123-654321
No	AD9710	£58.95	EALING Engines Design	Trevor Miles	01336-010107
No	AD9711	£290.00	HIRE Service Equipment	Nicole Webb	01875-558822
No	AD9712	£150.00	EUROBASE Co. Ltd	Sarah Star	01736-098765
No	AD9713	£135.00	AVON Construction	John Waters	01657-113355

Fig. 6.12 Results of the Unpaid Invoices Query

To save your newly created query, use the **File, Save As** command, and give it a name such as 'Unpaid invoices' in the Save As dialogue box. If you don't do this, you will be given the option to save the query when you close the Select Query results window above.

Once saved you can action this query whenever you like from the Database window, and get a current list of what unpaid invoices are outstanding at the time.

Types of Criteria

Access accepts the following expressions as criteria:

Arithmetic Operators		***Comparison Operators***		***Logical Operators***	
*	Multiply	<	Less than	And	And
/	Divide	<=	Less than or equal	Or	Inclusive or
+	Add	>	Greater than	Xor	Exclusive or
-	Subtract	>=	Greater than or equal	Not	Not equivalent
		=	Equal	Eqv	Equivalent
		<>	Not equal	Imp	Implication

Other operators		
Between	Between 50 And 150	All values between 50 and 150
In	In("Bath","Bristol")	All records with Bath and Bristol
Is	Is Null	All records with no value in that field
Like	Like "Brian *"	All records with Brian something in field
&	[Name]&" "&[Surname]	Concatenates strings

Using Wildcard Characters in Criteria

In an example on page 54 we used the criteria W* to mean any company whose name starts with the letter W. The asterisk in this criteria is known as a wildcard character.

To search for a pattern, you can use the asterisk (*) and the question mark (?) as wildcard characters when specifying criteria in expressions. An asterisk stands for any number of characters, while a question mark stands for any single character in the same position as the question mark.

The following examples show the use of wildcard characters in various types of expressions:

Entered Expression	*Meaning*	*Examples*
a?	Any two-letter word beginning with A	am, an, as, at
???d	Any four-letter word ending with d	find, hand, land yard
Sm?th	Any five-letter word beginning with Sm and ending with th	Smith Smyth
fie*	Any word starting with the letters fie	field, fiend, fierce, fiery
*ght	Any word ending with ght	alight, eight, fight, light, might, sight
*/5/99	All dates in May '99	1/5/99
a	Any word with the letter a in it	Brian, Mary, star, yard

Combining Criteria

By specifying additional criteria in a Query window you can create powerful queries for viewing your data. In the examples below we have added extra criteria to our Unpaid Invoices query.

To follow these on your PC just open the Query in Design view from the Database window.

The AND Criteria with Different Fields: When you insert criteria in several fields, but in the same row, Access assumes that you are searching for records that meet all of the criteria. In the next example (Fig. 6.13), the criteria should list the records with an Amount outstanding of between £50 and £150, and where the Contact name begins with 'M'. The second criteria can be entered as M*, and Access will convert this to Like "M*".

Field:	Paid?	InvoiceID	Amount	Name	Contact
Table:	Invoices	Invoices	Invoices	Customers	Customers
Sort:		Ascending			
Show:	☑	☑	☑	☑	☑
Criteria:	No		Between 50 And 100		Like "M*"
or:					

Unpaid invoices : Select Query

Paid?	Invoice No	Amount	Name	Contact	Phone
No	AD9703	£99.32	BARROWS Associates	Mandy Brown	01554-664422
No	AD9704	£55.98	STONEAGE Ltd	Mike Irons	01765-234567
No	AD9706	£68.52	WESTWOOD Ltd	Mary Slim	01234-667755

Record: 1 of 3

Fig. 6.13 Illustrating the AND Criteria with Different Fields

The OR Criteria with the Same Field: If you include multiple criteria in one field only, then Access assumes that you are searching for records that meet any one of the specified criteria. For example, the criteria <50 or >100 in the field Amount, shown in Fig. 6.14, list the required records, only if the No in the Paid? field is inserted in both rows.

Field:	Paid?	InvoiceID	Amount	Name	Contact
Table:	Invoices	Invoices	Invoices	Customers	Customers
Sort:		Ascending			
Show:	☑	☑	☑	☑	☑
Criteria:	No		<50		
or:	No		>100		

Unpaid invoices : Select Query

Paid?	Invoice No	Amount	Name	Contact	Phone
No	AD9701	£120.84	VORTEX Co. Ltd	Brian Storm	01776-223344
No	AD9705	£180.22	PARKWAY Gravel	James Stone	01534-987654
No	AD9707	£111.56	GLOWORM Ltd	Peter Summers	01432-746523
No	AD9709	£35.87	WORMGLAZE Ltd	Richard Glazer	01123-654321
No	AD9711	£290.00	HIRE Service Equipment	Nicole Webb	01875-558822
No	AD9712	£150.00	EUROBASE Co. Ltd	Sarah Star	01736-098765
No	AD9713	£135.00	AVON Construction	John Waters	01657-113355

Record: 1 of 7

Fig. 6.14 Illustrating the OR Criteria with the Same Field

The OR Criteria with Different Fields: If you include multiple criteria in different fields, but in different rows, then Access assumes that you are searching for records that meet either one or the other of the specified criteria. For example, the criteria Yes in the Paid? field and the criteria <50 in the Amount field, but in different rows, list the records shown in Fig. 6.15 on the next page.

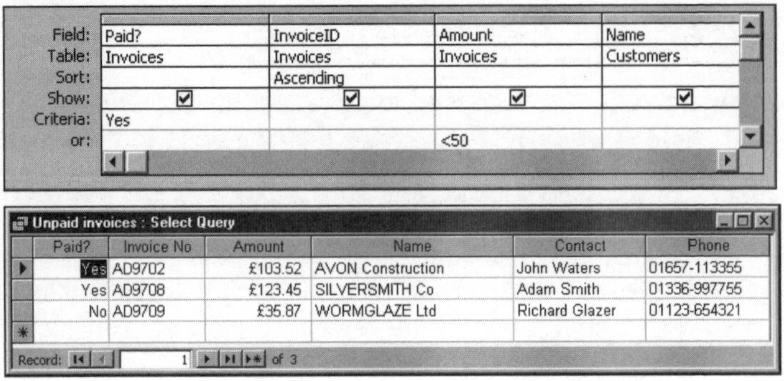

Field:	Paid?	InvoiceID	Amount	Name
Table:	Invoices	Invoices	Invoices	Customers
Sort:		Ascending		
Show:	☑	☑	☑	☑
Criteria:	Yes			
or:			<50	

Unpaid invoices : Select Query

Paid?	Invoice No	Amount	Name	Contact	Phone
Yes	AD9702	£103.52	AVON Construction	John Waters	01657-113355
Yes	AD9708	£123.45	SILVERSMITH Co	Adam Smith	01336-997755
No	AD9709	£35.87	WORMGLAZE Ltd	Richard Glazer	01123-654321

Record: 1 of 3

Fig. 6.15 Illustrating The OR Criteria with Different Fields

The AND and OR Criteria Together: The following choice of criteria will cause Access to retrieve either records that have Yes in the Paid? field and the company's name starts with the letter A, or records that the invoice amount is less than £50.

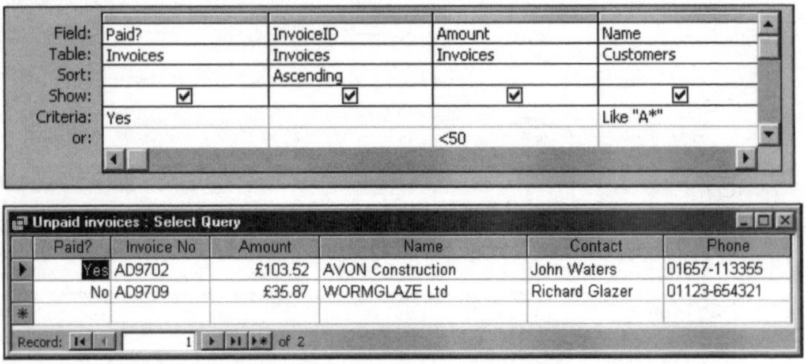

Field:	Paid?	InvoiceID	Amount	Name
Table:	Invoices	Invoices	Invoices	Customers
Sort:		Ascending		
Show:	☑	☑	☑	☑
Criteria:	Yes			Like "A*"
or:			<50	

Unpaid invoices : Select Query

Paid?	Invoice No	Amount	Name	Contact	Phone
Yes	AD9702	£103.52	AVON Construction	John Waters	01657-113355
No	AD9709	£35.87	WORMGLAZE Ltd	Richard Glazer	01123-654321

Record: 1 of 2

Fig. 6.16 Illustrating the AND and OR Criteria Together

Creating Calculated Fields

Let's assume that we want to increase the amounts payable on all invoices overdue by more than 30 days from today by 0.5%, as a penalty for not settling on time. We can achieve this by creating a calculated field in our database.

To create a calculated field, open **Adept 1**, click the Queries button in the Database window, select the Unpaid invoices query, and click the **Design** button on the Toolbar. Next, insert a field after the Amount field by highlighting the column after it and using the **Insert**, **Columns** command. Now type in the Field row of the newly inserted empty column, the following information:

```
New Amount:[Amount]*1.005
```

where *New Amount:* is our chosen name for the calculated field - the colon is essential. If you do not supply a name for the calculated field, Access uses the default name *Expr1:*, which you can rename later. The square brackets enclosing the word Amount in the above expression indicate a field name.

Next, click the **Properties** toolbar button, shown here, or use the **View, Properties** command, to set the Format property to Currency.

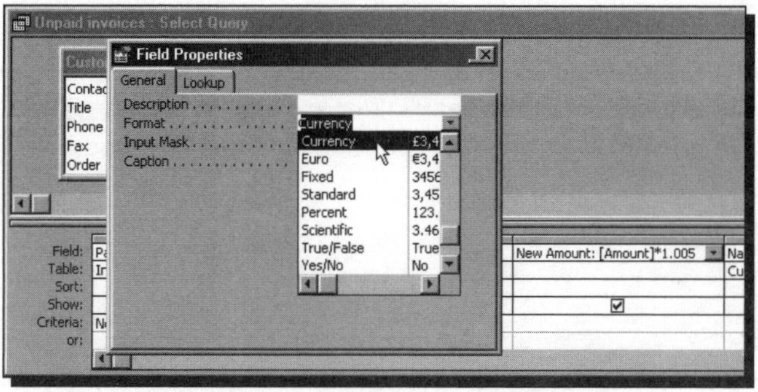

Fig. 6.17 Setting a Field's Properties to Currency

Finally, add the Date field from the Invoices table to our query and type the expression <#01/03/01# in its Criteria field - the hash marks and leading zeros will be supplied by Access if you do not type them in yourself.

Clicking either of the **Datasheet View**, or **Run**, buttons on the toolbar, displays the following results:

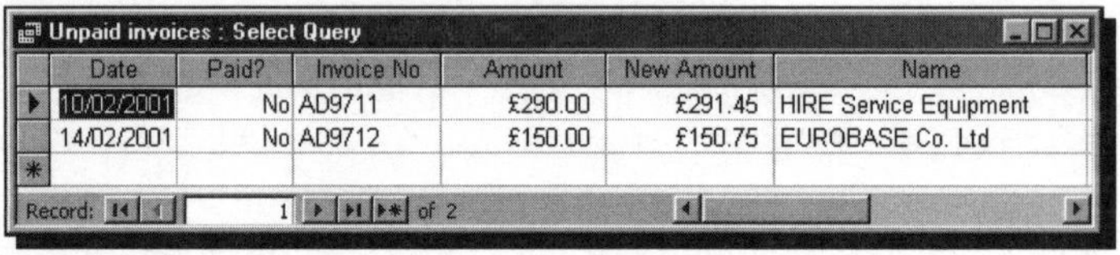
Unpaid invoices : Select Query

Date	Paid?	Invoice No	Amount	New Amount	Name
10/02/2001	No	AD9711	£290.00	£291.45	HIRE Service Equipment
14/02/2001	No	AD9712	£150.00	£150.75	EUROBASE Co. Ltd

Record: 1 of 2

Fig. 6.18 Results of the Penalty Invoices Query

We suggest you save this query under the name Penalty invoices.

Using Functions in Criteria

There are several functions that you can use in a calculated field of an Access query which can either be applied to extract information from text or date fields, or be used to calculate totals of entries.

Finding Part of a Text Field

Let us assume that you want to find information that is part of a text field, like the area code (first 5 numbers) in the Phone field of our Customers table. To help you search a table for only part of a text field, Access provides three string functions. The syntax of these functions is as follows:

```
Left(stringexpr,n)
Right(stringexpr,n)
Mid(stringexpr,start,n)
```

The *stringexpr* argument can be either a field name or a text expression, while *n* is the number of characters you are searching for, and *start* is the position of the first character you want to start from.

Thus, to extract the area code of the text field Phone in our Customers table, open the Unpaid Invoices query, click the Design View button on the toolbar, and type in the Field row of an empty field, either

```
Area Codes:Left([Phone],5)
```

or

```
Area Codes:Mid([Phone],1,5)
```

Note that to distinguish between the name of a field and a text expression, the name of the field is enclosed in square brackets.

Next, click the Datasheet View button on the toolbar. The result of such a query is displayed in Fig. 6.19 below.

Unpaid invoices : Select Query

Paid?	Invoice No	Amount	Name	Contact	Phone	Area Codes
No	AD9701	£120.84	VORTEX Co. Ltd	Brian Storm	01776-223344	01776
No	AD9703	£99.32	BARROWS Associates	Mandy Brown	01554-664422	01554
No	AD9704	£55.98	STONEAGE Ltd	Mike Irons	01765-234567	01765
No	AD9705	£180.22	PARKWAY Gravel	James Stone	01534-987654	01534
No	AD9706	£68.52	WESTWOOD Ltd	Mary Slim	01234-667755	01234
No	AD9707	£111.56	GLOWORM Ltd	Peter Summers	01432-746523	01432
No	AD9709	£35.87	WORMGLAZE Ltd	Richard Glazer	01123-654321	01123
No	AD9710	£58.95	EALING Engines Design	Trevor Miles	01336-010107	01336
No	AD9711	£290.00	HIRE Service Equipment	Nicole Webb	01875-558822	01875
No	AD9712	£150.00	EUROBASE Co. Ltd	Sarah Star	01736-098765	01736
No	AD9713	£135.00	AVON Construction	John Waters	01657-113355	01657

Record: 1 of 11

Fig. 6.19 Results of the Area Codes Query

Finding Part of a Date Field

To extract part of a date field, such as the month in which unpaid invoices were issued, type

```
Month:DatePart("m",[Date])
```

in the Field row of an empty field.

To extract the year in which unpaid invoices were issued, type

```
Year:DatePart("yyyy",[Date])
```

in the Field row of an empty field. This function returns the year in four digits, such as 2001.

The result of such a query is shown in Fig. 6.20 below.

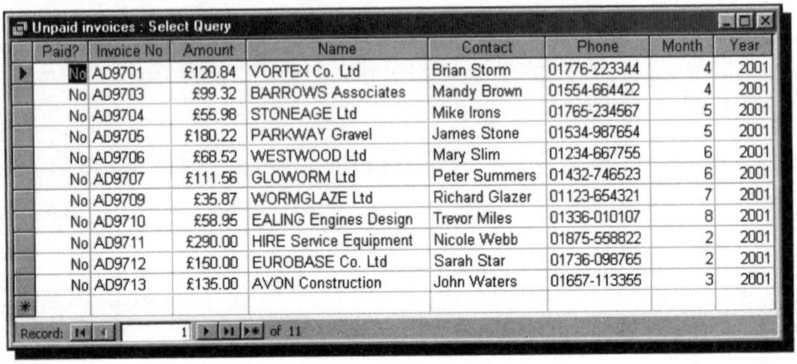

Unpaid invoices : Select Query

Paid?	Invoice No	Amount	Name	Contact	Phone	Month	Year
No	AD9701	£120.84	VORTEX Co. Ltd	Brian Storm	01776-223344	4	2001
No	AD9703	£99.32	BARROWS Associates	Mandy Brown	01554-664422	4	2001
No	AD9704	£55.98	STONEAGE Ltd	Mike Irons	01765-234567	5	2001
No	AD9705	£180.22	PARKWAY Gravel	James Stone	01534-987654	5	2001
No	AD9706	£68.52	WESTWOOD Ltd	Mary Slim	01234-667755	6	2001
No	AD9707	£111.56	GLOWORM Ltd	Peter Summers	01432-746523	6	2001
No	AD9709	£35.87	WORMGLAZE Ltd	Richard Glazer	01123-654321	7	2001
No	AD9710	£58.95	EALING Engines Design	Trevor Miles	01336-010107	8	2001
No	AD9711	£290.00	HIRE Service Equipment	Nicole Webb	01875-558822	2	2001
No	AD9712	£150.00	EUROBASE Co. Ltd	Sarah Star	01736-098765	2	2001
No	AD9713	£135.00	AVON Construction	John Waters	01657-113355	3	2001

Record: 1 of 11

Fig. 6.20 Results of the Date Queries

Calculating Totals in Queries

It is possible that you might want to know the total value of outstanding invoices grouped by month. Access allows you to perform calculations on groups of records using *totals* queries, also known as *aggregate* queries.

Function	***Used to Find***
Avg	The average of values in a field
Count	The number of values in a field
First	The field value from the first record in a table or query
Last	The field value from the last record in a table or query
Max	The highest value in a field
Min	The lowest value in a field
StDev	The standard deviation of values in a field
Sum	The total of values in a field
Var	The variance of values in a field

The table on the previous page lists the functions that can be used in queries to display totals. These functions are entered in the Totals row of a query which can be displayed by clicking the **Totals** button, shown here, while in Design View.

In Fig. 6.21 below, we show the one-table query to find the total value of unpaid invoices grouped by month.

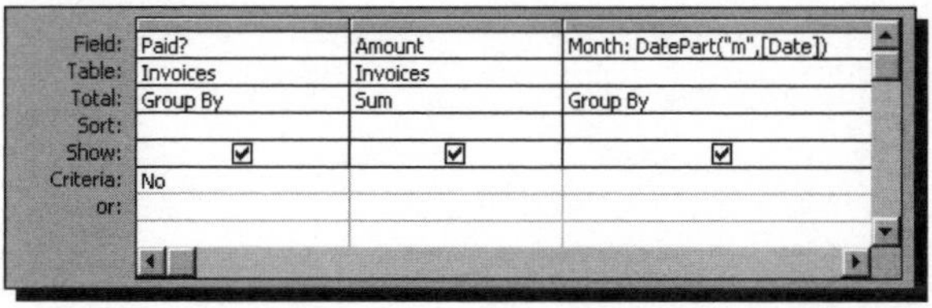

Fig. 6.21 Using the Sum Total Function in a Query

The retrieved records from such a query are shown in Fig. 6.22 below. We have named this query 'Monthly invoices'.

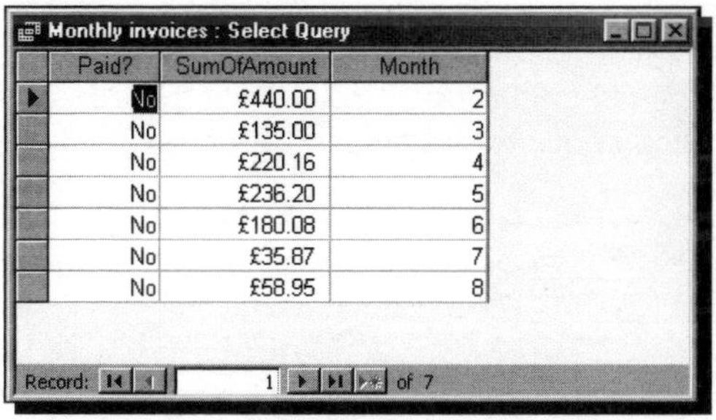

Monthly invoices : Select Query
Paid? | SumOfAmount | Month
No | £440.00 | 2
No | £135.00 | 3
No | £220.16 | 4
No | £236.20 | 5
No | £180.08 | 6
No | £35.87 | 7
No | £58.95 | 8
Record: 1 of 7

Fig. 6.22 Results of the Monthly Invoices Query

7

More Advanced Queries

In the last chapter we saw how to create a query with fields taken from two tables. The query in question was Unpaid invoices, shown in Fig. 7.1 below in Design view.

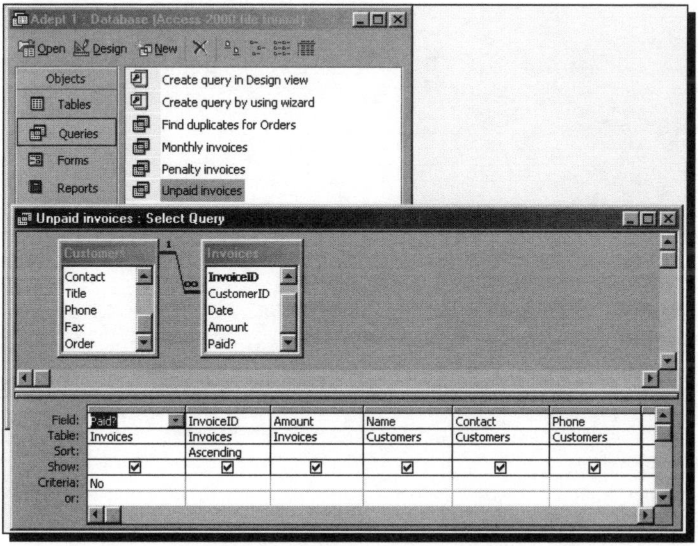

Fig. 7.1 The Unpaid invoices Query in Design View

To make it easier to see which field in the above query comes from which table, Access displays the name of the table by default. This option is controlled from the **View, Table Names** command when in Design view. When this menu option is ticked, Access adds the Table row in the QBE grid, as shown in Fig. 7.1 above.

Now, suppose we would like to add the Orders table so that we can see the OrderID field in the extracted records of our query. To do this, click the **Show Table** button, shown here, which opens the Show Table dialogue box we saw earlier in Fig. 6.10. In this box, select Orders and click the **Add** button, then drag the OrderID field onto the QBE grid, as shown in Fig. 7.2 below.

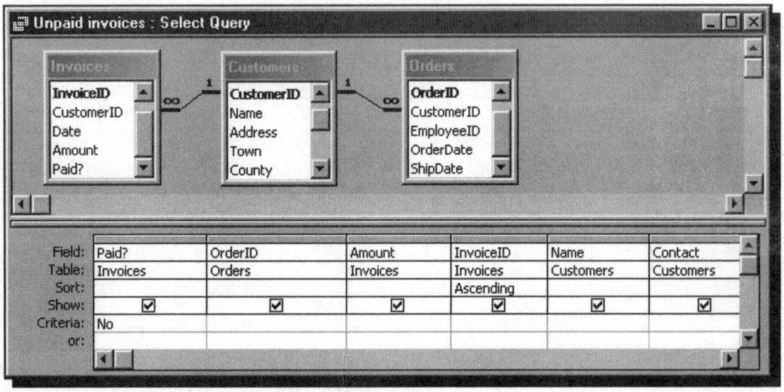

Fig. 7.2 The OrderID Field Added to the Query Grid

To find out what type of join exists between two tables, click the join line to highlight it, as shown here in Fig. 7.3, then right-click and select **Join Properties** from the shortcut menu. This will open the following dialogue box, in which we need option 2. Select it so that the Query will extract the correct records.

Fig. 7.3 Join Shortcut Menu

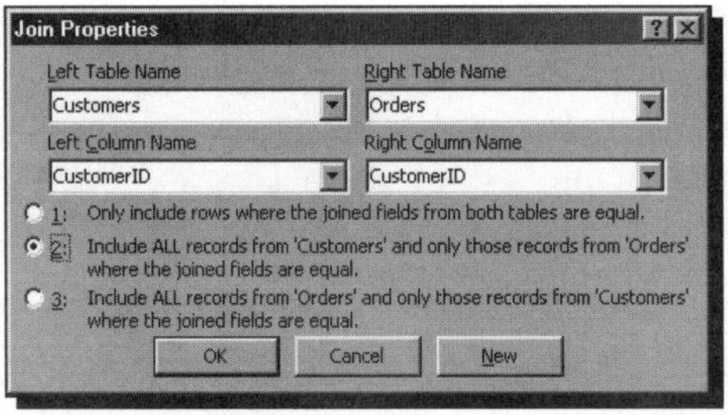

Fig. 7.4 The Join Properties Dialogue Box

Types of Joins

Microsoft Access supports the following types of joins:

Join Types	Effect
Equi-joins or Inner joins	A join in which records from two tables are combined and added to a dynaset only when there are equal values in the joined fields. For example, you can find records that show orders placed by each customer, with the dynaset containing only records for customers who have placed orders.
Outer joins	A join in which all the records from one table are added to the dynaset, and only those records from the other table for which values in the joined fields are equal. For example, you can find records that show all customers together with any orders they have placed.
Self-joins	A join in which records from one table are combined with other records from the same table when there are matching values in the joined fields. A self-join can be an equi-join or an outer join.

For an inner join, select option 1 from the Join Properties dialogue box. For an outer join, select option 2 or 3, depending on which records you want to include.

For example, choosing option 2 (also called a *left outer join*), displays all the required records from the Customers table and only those records from Orders where the joined fields are equal. Option 3 (also called a *right outer join*), on the other hand, attempts to display all records in Orders and only those records from Customers where the joined fields are equal, resulting in some confusion in our particular example.

Creating a Parameter Query

A *Parameter Query* is a variation of the *Select Query* - the type we have been using so far. A Parameter Query is used when you frequently run the same query, but need to change the criteria each time you run it. Instead of having to make changes to the QBE grid, the design of a Parameter Query forces Access to prompt you for criteria. This type of query is particularly useful when used as a filter with forms.

To design a Parameter Query, design a **New** query in the normal way (do not use the Query Wizards), or change an existing Select Query. We have chosen the latter route and selected to change the Penalty invoices query. In Design view, this now looks as follows:

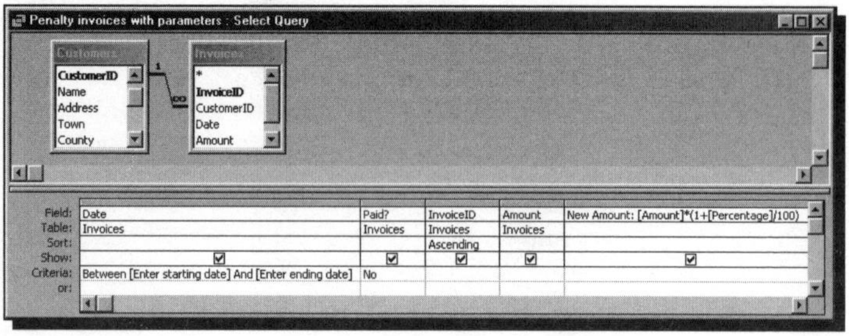

Fig. 7.5 A Parameter Query

Note the two changes made to the original query. In the Date field we have entered two prompts (in square brackets) in the Criteria row, namely

```
[Enter starting date]
[Enter ending date]
```

and in the calculated field we have replaced the *1.005 by

```
*(1+[Percentage]/100)
```

When working with expressions like these, that are longer than the visible cell space available, it is often easier to use the Zoom window opened into the cell with the <Shift+**F2**> key strokes.

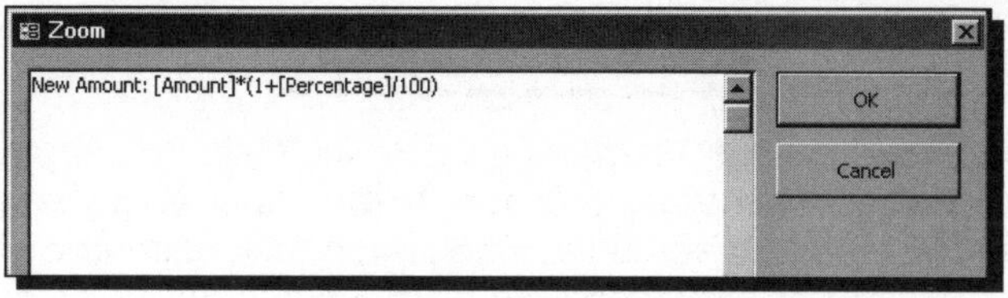

Fig. 7.6 Using a Zoom Window

When this query is run, Access asks for input values in three successive Enter Parameter Value boxes, as shown in Fig. 7.7 below.

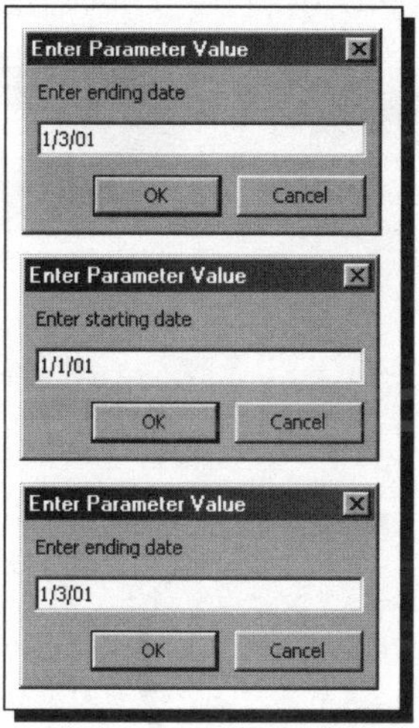

Fig. 7.7 Entering the Three Parameters into the Query

Providing the appropriate input information, displays the result of the search, as follows:

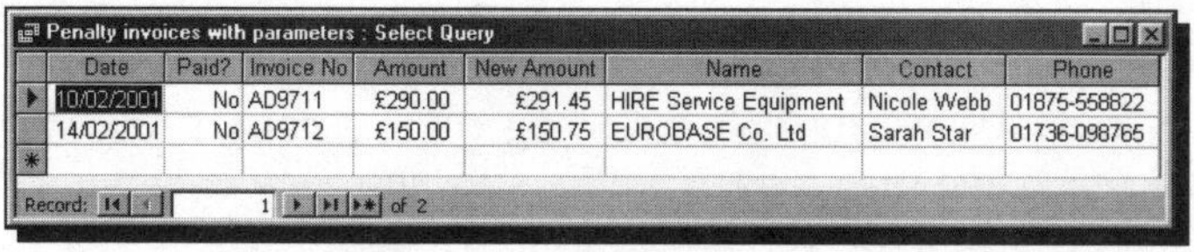

Date	Paid?	Invoice No	Amount	New Amount	Name	Contact	Phone
10/02/2001	No	AD9711	£290.00	£291.45	HIRE Service Equipment	Nicole Webb	01875-558822
14/02/2001	No	AD9712	£150.00	£150.75	EUROBASE Co. Ltd	Sarah Star	01736-098765

Fig. 7.8 The Query Results

We have saved this query under the name ‘Penalty invoices with parameters’.

Creating a Crosstab Query

You create a *Crosstab Query* to display totals in a compact, spreadsheet format. A Crosstab query can present a large amount of summary data in a more readable form. The layout of the extracted data from such a query is ideal as the basis for a report.

For example, suppose we wanted to examine which of our employees was responsible for our customers' orders in each month. The information is contained in the Orders table of our database as shown in Fig. 7.9 below

Orders : Table

Order ID	Customer ID	Employee ID	Order Date	Ship Date
97085VOR	VORT	A.D. Smith	20/01/2001	10/02/2001
97097AVO	AVON	W.A. Brown	25/01/2001	14/02/2001
97099BAR	BARR	S.F. Adams	01/02/2001	02/03/2001
97002STO	STON	C.H. Wills	20/02/2001	25/04/2001
97006PAR	PARK	A.D. Smith	13/03/2001	16/04/2001
97010WES	WEST	W.A. Brown	15/03/2001	26/04/2001
97018GLO	GLOW	L.S. Stevens	25/04/2001	19/05/2001
97025SIL	SILV	S.F. Adams	28/04/2001	22/05/2001
97029WOR	WORM	C.H. Wills	20/05/2001	13/06/2001
97039EAL	EALI	A.D. Smith	30/05/2001	25/06/2001
97045HIR	HIRE	W.A. Brown	18/06/2001	08/07/2001
97051EUR	EURO	L.S. Stevens	25/06/2001	19/07/2001
97064AVO	AVON	S.F. Adams	20/07/2001	15/08/2001

Record: 1 of 13

Fig. 7.9 The Orders Table Sorted on Order Date

From the way this information is presented it is very difficult to work out who was responsible for which order in a given month. However, a Crosstab query that lists the names of the employees in rows and each month as a column heading, would be an ideal way to present this type of information.

To create a Crosstab query, open the **Adept 1** database and click first the Queries button, then the **New** button in the Database window. Next, select the **Crosstab Query Wizard** option from the list on the New Query dialogue box, as shown in Fig. 7.10 on the next page.

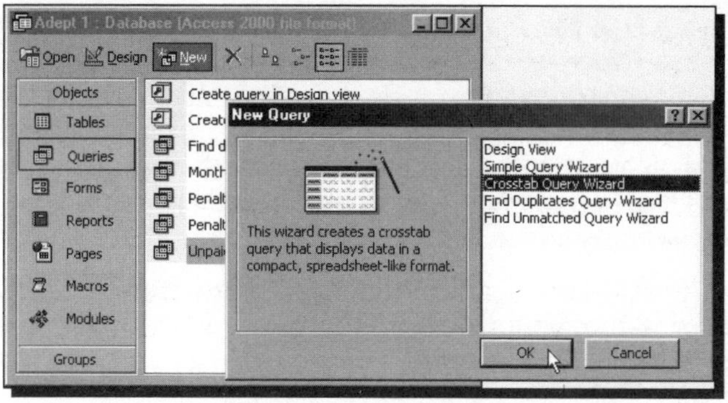

Fig. 7.10 Starting the Crosstab Query Wizard

Pressing the **OK** button, opens the first Crosstab Query Wizard dialogue box. From this, select Orders from the displayed list of **Tables** and press the **Next** button.

From the next dialogue box, shown in Fig. 7.11 below, select a maximum of three fields from the displayed list, which will become the row headings of the crosstab form. Choose OrderID, CustomerID, and EmployeeID, in that order. The order you select these fields is important as Access will list the results of the query in alphabetical order of the first selected field.

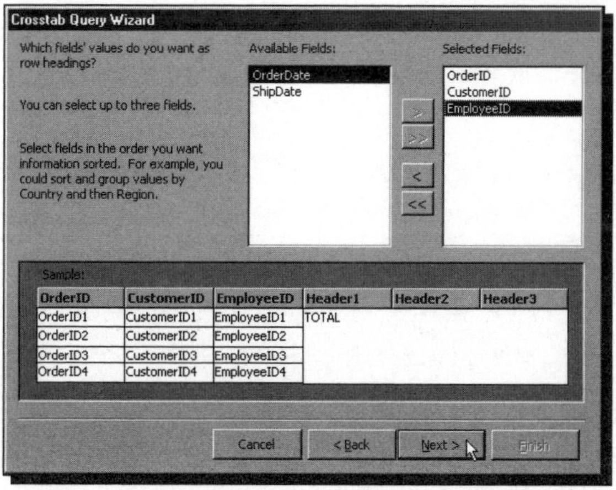

Fig. 7.11 Selecting Fields for the Crosstab Query

Having selected the three fields, click the **Next** button, and choose OrderDate as the field whose value you want as the column headings. Press **Next**, select Month as the time interval by which you want to group your columns and press **Next** again. On the following dialogue box choose Count from the **Functions** list and press **Next**. Finally, accept the default name for the query, and press **Finish**.

The results of this Crosstab query are shown in Fig. 7.12 below with column widths set to Best Fit so that you can see the whole year at a glance.

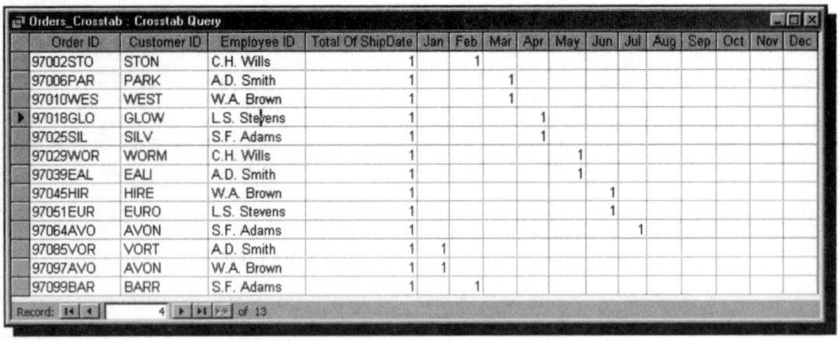

Order ID	Customer ID	Employee ID	Total Of ShipDate	Jan	Feb	Mar	Apr	May	Jun	Jul	Aug	Sep	Oct	Nov	Dec
97002STO	STON	C.H. Wills	1		1										
97006PAR	PARK	A.D. Smith	1			1									
97010WES	WEST	W.A. Brown	1			1									
97018GLO	GLOW	L.S. Stevens	1				1								
97025SIL	SILV	S.F. Adams	1				1								
97029WOR	WORM	C.H. Wills	1					1							
97039EAL	EALI	A.D. Smith	1					1							
97045HIR	HIRE	W.A. Brown	1						1						
97051EUR	EURO	L.S. Stevens	1						1						
97064AVO	AVON	S.F. Adams	1							1					
97085VOR	VORT	A.D. Smith	1	1											
97097AVO	AVON	W.A. Brown	1	1											
97099BAR	BARR	S.F. Adams	1		1										

Fig. 7.12 The Crosstab Query Results

As you can see from the above screen, the required information is tabulated and is extremely easy to read. However, the displayed recordset is not updatable.

To see the underlying structure of the query, click the **Design View** button to display the QBE grid, as follows:

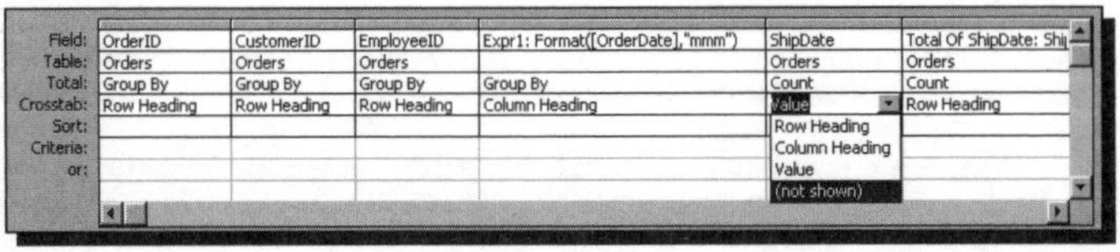

Field:	OrderID	CustomerID	EmployeeID	Expr1: Format([OrderDate],"mmm")	ShipDate	Total Of ShipDate: Shi
Table:	Orders	Orders	Orders		Orders	Orders
Total:	Group By	Group By	Group By	Group By	Count	Count
Crosstab:	Row Heading	Row Heading	Row Heading	Column Heading	Value	Row Heading
Sort:						
Criteria:						
or:						

Fig. 7.13 The Crosstab Query in Design View

If you want to use a field for grouping, sorting, or setting criteria, but to exclude the field from the recordset, click the arrow in that field's Crosstab cell, and select **(not shown)** from the displayed list, as shown in Fig. 7.13 above.

Creating Queries for Updating Records

When a query is based on either a single table or on two tables with a one-to-one relationship, all the fields in the query are updatable.

Queries which include more than one table, when some of the tables have a one-to-many relationship, are more difficult to design so that they are updatable.

The easiest way of finding out whether you can update records from a query, is to design the query, run it and try to change values in its various fields and also add data. If the table is updateable Access will let you make these changes, if not you will simply not be allowed to edit it.

All other types of queries, such as a Crosstab query, a query with totals, a query with Unique Values property set to Yes, a Union query, a Pass-through query, a calculated or read-only field, can not be used to update data.

To find out more, we suggest you look up the 'When can I update data from a query?' section in Access Help, as shown in Fig. 7.14.

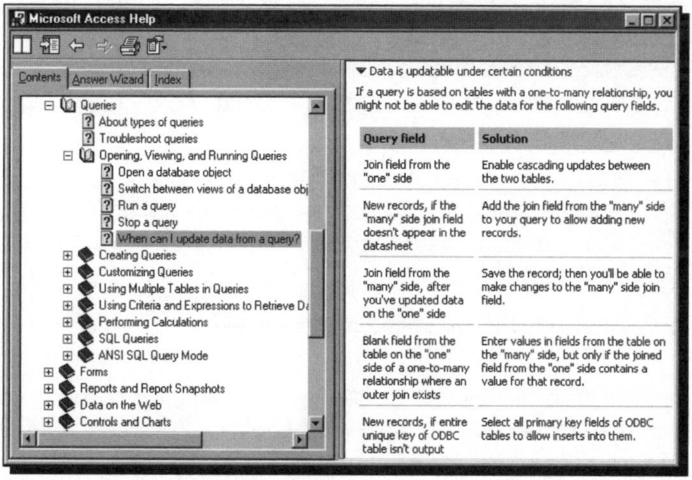

Fig. 7.14 When can I update data from a query?

Creating Action Queries

You can create *Action Queries* in the same way as Select Queries. Action Queries are used to make bulk changes to data rather than simply displaying data. For this reason, Action Queries can be dangerous for the novice, simply because they change your database.

There are four different types of Action Queries, with the following functions:

Type of Query	***Function***
Append query	Adds records from one or more tables to another table or tables.
Delete query	Deletes records from a table or tables.
Make-table query	Creates a new table from all or part of another table or tables.
Update query	Changes the data in a group of records

In an earlier version of Access, you could quickly create an Action query which moved old orders to an Old Orders Archive table, by using the Archive Query Wizard. If you want to design such a query from scratch, then we suggest you go through the following steps:

- Use a Make-table query to copy selected records from an existing table into a new table, named, say, Old Orders Archive.
- Change the design of the Make-table query so that on subsequent execution of the query it Appends selected records from your original table to the Old Orders Archive table.
- Use the Delete query to delete the archived records from the original table.

In what follows, we will go through the steps necessary to create an Old Orders Archive query.

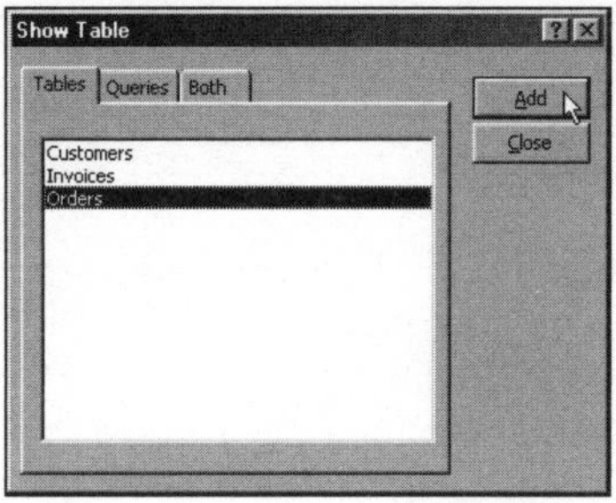

Fig. 7.15 The Show Table Box

Open the database **Adept 1** and first click the **Queries** button in the Database window, then double-click on the **Create query in Design view** option.

In the Show Table dialogue box that opens next (Fig. 7.15), select Orders, as shown here, then press the **Add** button, followed by the **Close** button. This adds the Orders table to the Select Query window which also contains the QBE grid, so that you can design an appropriate query.

Drag all the fields from the Orders table onto the QBE grid, and add in the OrderDate field the criteria <=4/4/01, as shown in Fig. 7.16 below.

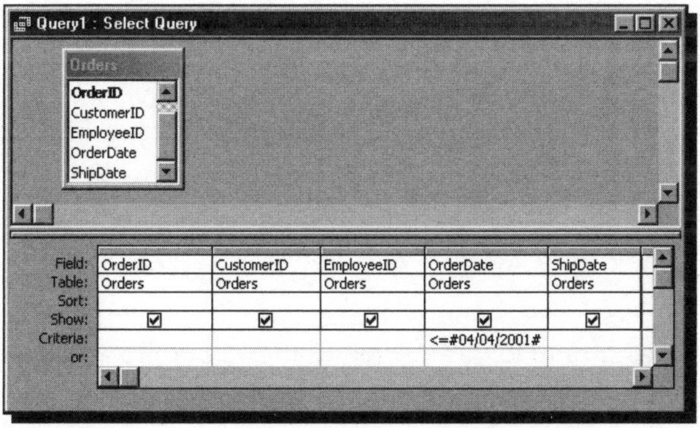

Fig. 7.16 Creating a Make-Table Query

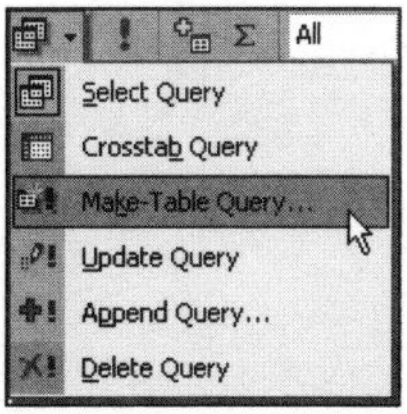

Fig. 7.17 The Query Type Button Menu

Click the arrow next to the **Query Type** button on the toolbar, shown in Fig. 7.17, which displays the available query types. Select the **Make-Table Query** option which opens the Make Table dialogue box shown in Fig. 7.18 overleaf.

Finally, type the name of the new table, say, Old Orders Archive, and press **OK**.

Fig. 7.18 The Make Table Dialogue Box

If you press the **Run** toolbar button a warning box is displayed. In our example, we are told that six records are about to be pasted onto our new table, as shown in Fig. 7.19.

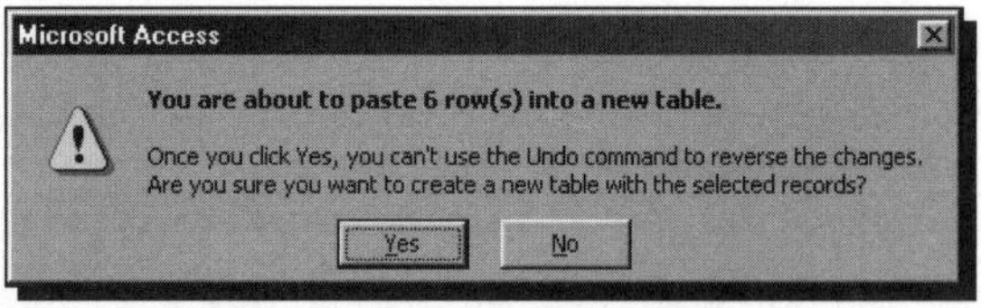

Fig. 7.19 An Access Warning Message

Pressing **Yes**, copies the selected records from the Orders table to the newly created Old Orders Archive table.

Next, action the **Query**, **Append Query** menu command. The Append dialogue box is displayed with the Old Orders Archive name appearing as default. Press **OK** and close the Append Query window. When you click the 'X' button to close the Append Query window, you will be asked whether you would like your design to be saved. Select **Yes**, and in the displayed Save As dialogue box, type the new name for the query. We chose to call it Append to Old Orders Archive.

As an exercise, you could go through the steps of designing another Make Table query, but select the Delete option of the Query Type menu. This would be used to delete old records from the Orders table once they have been moved to the Old Orders Archive table.

Before you do this, the next time you look at the Database window you should see that Access has placed a new query in the Query list, as shown in Fig. 7.20 below. This has an exclamation mark attached to its icon so that you don't run it inadvertently.

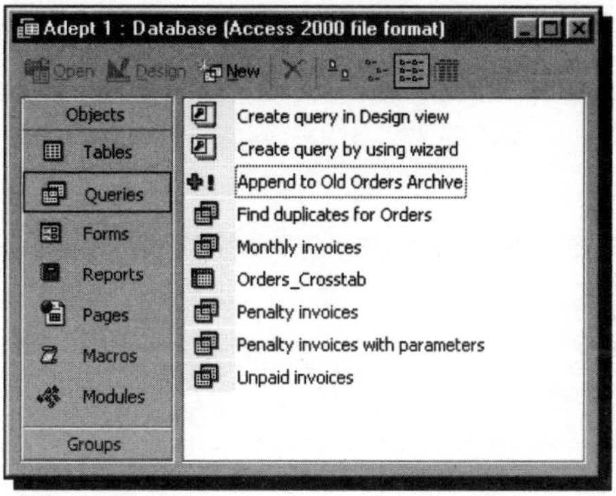

Fig. 7.20 The New Action Query in the Database Window Listing

In all, there are four Action queries available in Access, with the following functions.

1 The **Make-Table** query; used to create a table by retrieving the records that meet certain criteria and using them to create a new table.

2 The **Append** query; used to append (add) records from one table to another existing table.

3 The **Update** query; used to change data in existing tables, such as the cost per hour charged to your customers.

4 The **Delete** query; used to delete (remove) records that meet certain pre-defined criteria from a table.

Help on Queries

As we are sure you have found by now, the Help section of Access is essential reading when you are tackling a new section. We strongly recommend that you work your way through the section on Queries.

Below is a typical example of the depth of detail in some of the Help screens.

▼ Dates

Expression	Result
#2/2/2000#	For a ShippedDate field, orders shipped on February 2, 2000 (ANSI-89)
'2/2/2000'	For a ShippedDate field, orders shipped on February 2, 2000 (ANSI-92)
Date()	For a RequiredDate field, orders for today's date
Between Date( ) And DateAdd("M", 3, Date( ))	For a RequiredDate field, orders required between today's date and three months from today's date
< Date( ) - 30	For an OrderDate field, orders more than 30 days old
Year([OrderDate]) = 1999	For an OrderDate field, orders with order dates in 1999
DatePart("q", [OrderDate]) = 4	For an OrderDate field, orders for the fourth calendar quarter
DateSerial(Year ([OrderDate]), Month ([OrderDate]) + 1, 1) - 1	For an OrderDate field, orders for the last day of each month
Year([OrderDate]) = Year(Now()) And Month([OrderDate]) = Month(Now())	For an OrderDate field, orders for the current year and month

Fig. 7.21 A Help Page of Date Expressions

8

Using Forms

We saw on page 55 how easy it was to create a single column form to view our Customers table. To see this again, open **Adept 1** and in the Database window click the **Form** button, then double-click on Customers, which should display the following:

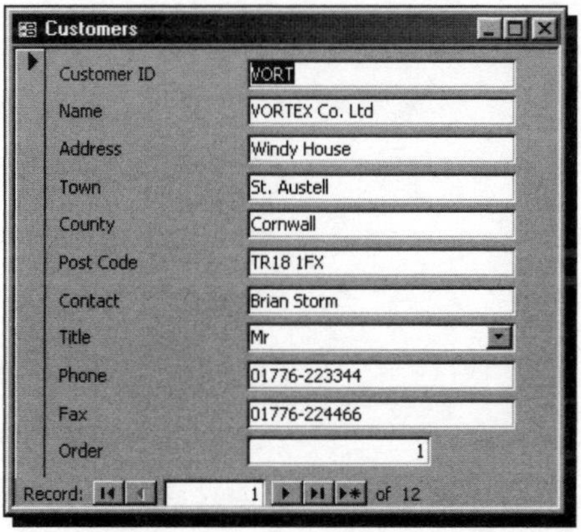

Fig. 8.1 The Automatically Created Customers Form

You can use forms to find, edit, and add data in a convenient manner - many people find them easier to work with than tables. Access provides you with an easy way of designing various types of forms, some of which are discussed here. Forms look good on screen, but do not produce very good output on paper, whereas reports, covered in the next chapter, are designed to look good on paper, but do not necessarily look good on screen.

Using the Form Wizard

Using the Form Wizard, you can easily display data from either a table or a query in Form view.

Open the **Adept 1** database, and in the Database window click the Forms button, then the **New** button which opens the New Form dialogue box in which you must choose either a table or a query on which to base the new form. In the screen dump below, we chose Form Wizard and the Customers table, before we clicked the **OK** button.

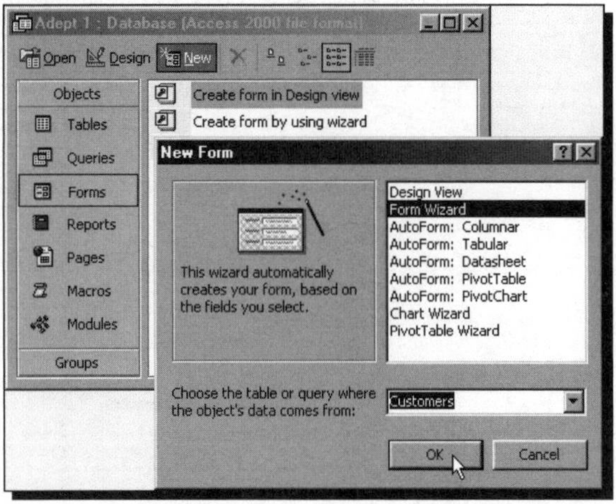

Fig. 8.2 The New Form Box Options

Creating a Form with a Subform

To help us enter new invoice data into our **Adept 1** database we will build a new form which holds the fields from the Customers table, but has a subform holding the Invoices table. So when the main form shows all the details of a particular customer, the subform will be visible with all the invoice information for that customer.

Before doing this you must make sure that your table relationships have been set up correctly. In our example, as long as you have followed our instructions, there should not be too many problems!

In the first wizard dialogue box, shown in Fig. 8.3 below, the table Customers should already be selected from the list. The two tables we are going to use have a one-to-many relationship, and Customers is the 'one' side of this one-to-many relationship. In other words, every customer can have many invoices raised, but each invoice will only be relevant to one customer.

Double-click all the fields except Order in the **Available Fields** list to move them to the **Selected Fields** box, as shown.

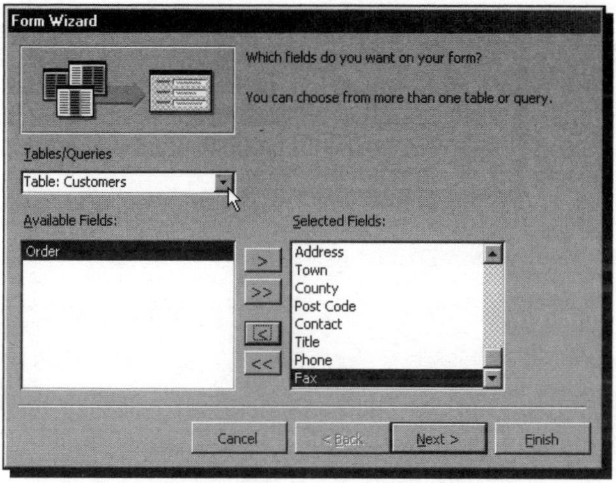

Fig. 8.3 The First Form Wizard Dialogue Box

In the **same** wizard dialogue box, select the Invoices table from the **Tables/Queries** list and select all the fields except CustomerID, then click the **Next** button.

As long as you have set up the relationships correctly before starting the procedure, the next wizard box (Fig. 8.4), asks which table or query you want to view by. In our case to create the Customers form, click **by Customers**. In the same dialogue box, select the **Form with subform(s)** option, as shown on the next page and click the **Next** button.

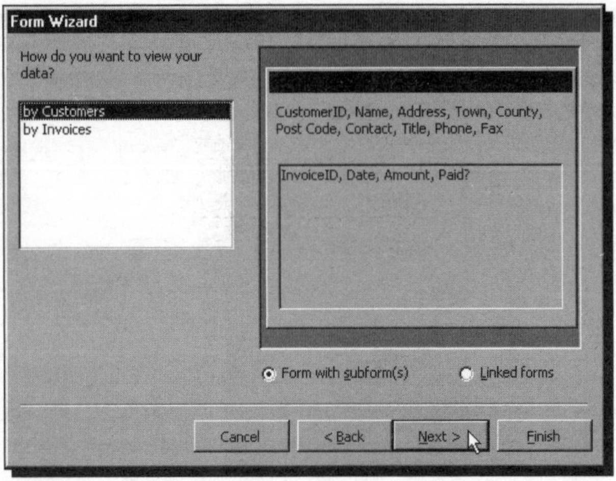

Fig. 8.4 The Second Form Wizard Box

Select **Datasheet** layout and Standard style in the next two wizard dialogue boxes (not shown here), and name the **Form** Customer Invoice Details in the last box, shown in Fig. 8.5.

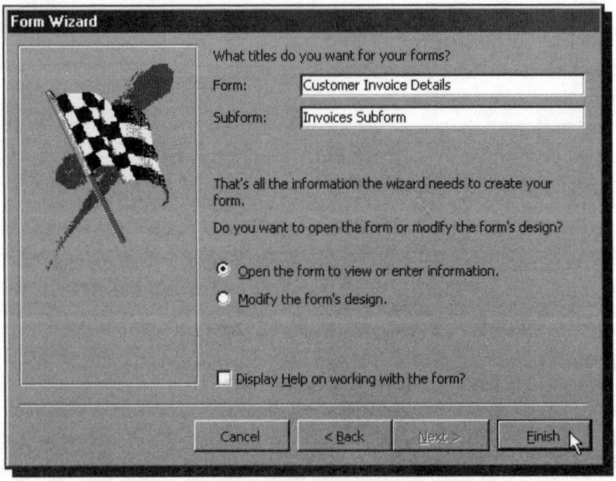

Fig. 8.5 The Last Form Wizard Dialogue Box

When you click **Finish**, Access creates two forms, one for the main form and subform control, and one for the subform, and opens the new form shown in Fig. 8.6.

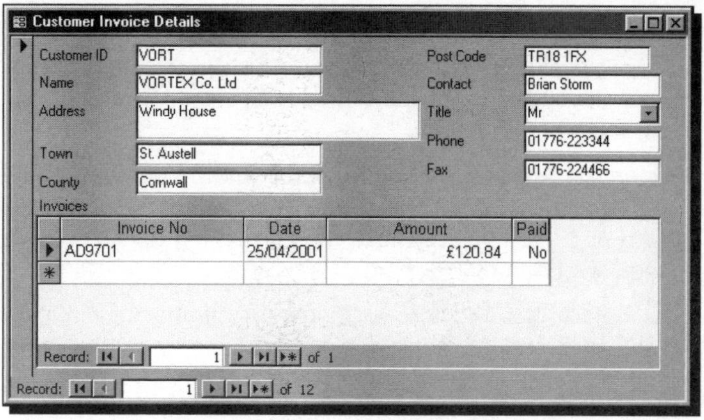

Fig. 8.6 The New Form with a Subform Included

It's as easy as that with Access 2002. The form produced almost automatically is by no means perfect, but for most people would be adequate. We will customise it later on.

The other Form Wizards available are:

AutoForm: Columnar - Creates a columnar form with all the field labels appearing in the first column and the data in the second. The form displays one record at a time.

AutoForm: Tabular - Tabulates a screen full of records in tabular form with the field labels appearing at the head of each column.

AutoForm: Datasheet - Similar to the Tabular form, but in worksheet display format.

AutoForm: PivotTable - Lets you dynamically change the layout of the form to analyse data in different ways.

AutoForm: PivotChart - Similar to the PivotTable form, but displays data in graphical chart form.

Chart Wizard - Displays data graphically.

PivotTable Wizard - Creates a form with an Excel PivotTable - an interactive table that can summarise data using the format and calculation methods specified by the user.

Creating a Chart Form

As another example of using the Form Wizard we will step through the process of building a chart form to graphically show some of our data.

Open the **Adept 1** database, and in the Database window click the Forms button, then the **New** button, select Chart Wizard and the Invoices table, before clicking the **OK** button on the New Form dialogue box.

As before, the Wizard will display a number of dialogue boxes, after making appropriate selections, click the **Next** button to progress through the automatic design of the new form.

To continue with our example, the Wizard displays the first dialogue box, shown in Fig. 8.7, in which you are asked to specify the fields that contain the data you want to chart.

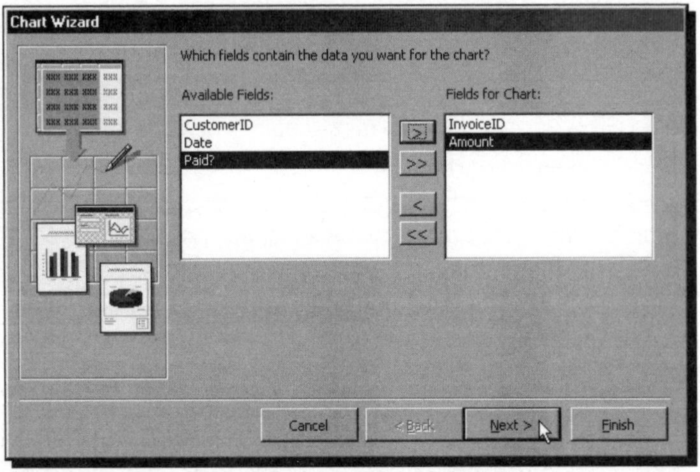

Fig. 8.7 The First Chart Wizard Dialogue Box

We chose InvoiceID and Amount, and then pressed **Next**. This opens the next wizard box in which you are asked what type of chart you would like. We chose Bar Chart, the first one on the second row before pressing **Next**, as shown in Fig. 8.8 on the next page.

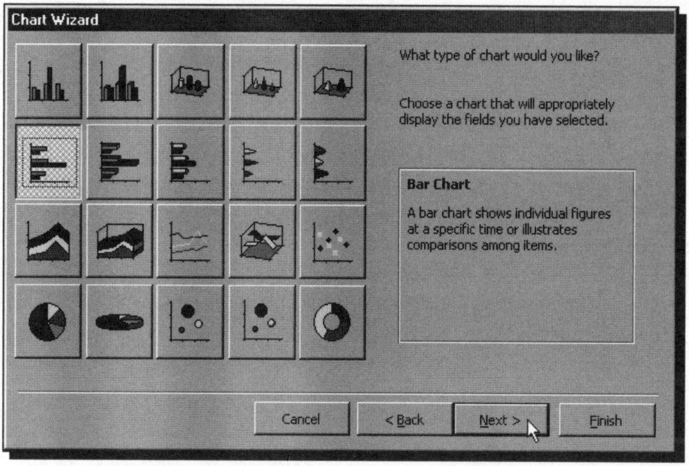

Fig. 8.8 The Second Chart Wizard Dialogue Box

In the following dialogue box, shown in Fig. 8.9, double-click the x-axis button (the one with the caption 'SumOfAmount') and select 'None' from the list in the displayed Summarize dialogue box, shown below, and press **OK**, followed by the **Next** button.

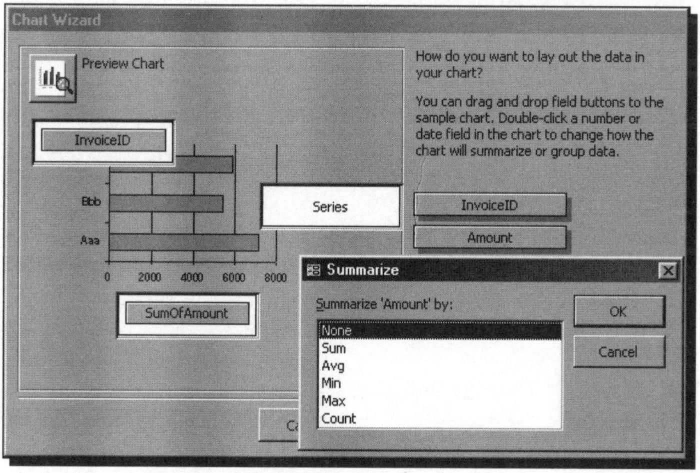

Fig. 8.9 Controlling the Layout of the Chart

In the last dialogue box, not shown here, the Wizard then asks you what title to give to the form - we chose 'Invoice Amounts'.

Pressing the **Finish** button, allows the Wizard to display the final result, shown in Fig. 8.10 below. It is as easy as that to get a graphical view of the amounts involved in each of your invoices. When asked, we named the form 'Invoice Chart' before closing it.

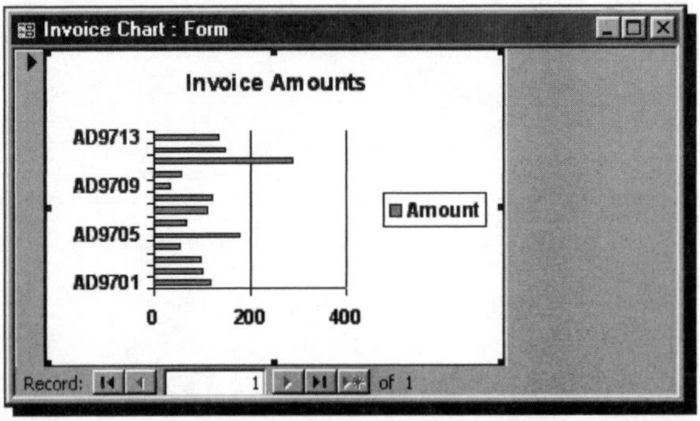

Fig. 8.10 A Bar Chart on an Access Form

You have probably realised by now that Access saves any changes to the data in a database automatically as soon as they are made. Changes to the design of the database or to any of its components, however, are a different thing. You have to save these yourself. This is easily done, either with

the **File**, **Save** menu command, or by clicking the **Save** toolbar button shown here.

Customising a Form

You can customise a form by changing the appearance of text, data, and any other attributes. In Fig. 8.11 below we show a slightly modified version of the Customer Invoice Details form in Design view. It is in this view that you make any changes to the design.

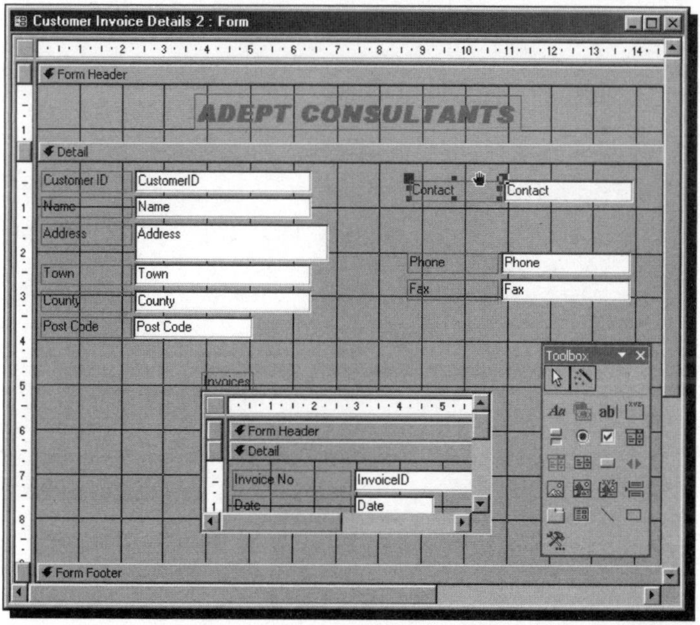

Fig. 8.11 Our Customised Form in Design View

As you can see, a form in Design view is made up of boxes, or controls, attached to a grid. Clicking in the Contact box, for example, causes markers to appear around it as shown above. When the mouse pointer is then placed within either the label box or data box, it changes to a hand which indicates that you can drag the box to a new position. This method moves both label and data boxes together.

If you look more closely at the markers around the label and data boxes, you will see that they are of different size, as shown next in Fig. 8.12.

Fig. 8.12 A Selected Label and Data Box

The larger square markers are 'move' handles, while the smaller ones are 'size' handles. In the above example you can use the 'move' handles of either the label or the data box to move one independently of the other.

Boxes on a form can be made larger or smaller by simply pointing to the sizing handles and dragging them in the appropriate direction.

The Form/Report Toolbar

You can further customise any form (or report) features, using the various buttons that appear on the Form/Report toolbar when forms or reports are active in Design view. The toolbar is shown here in two tiers.

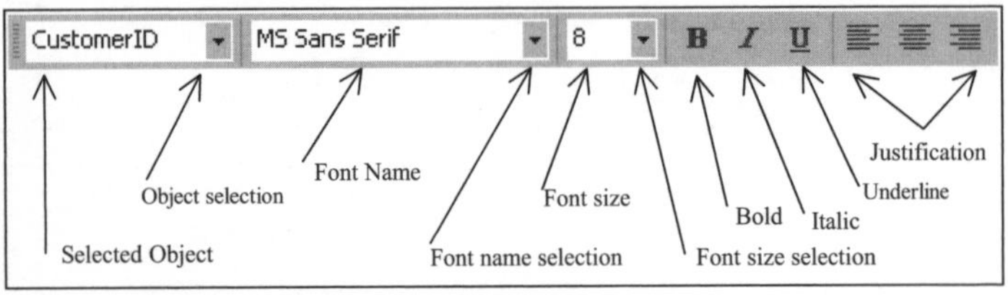

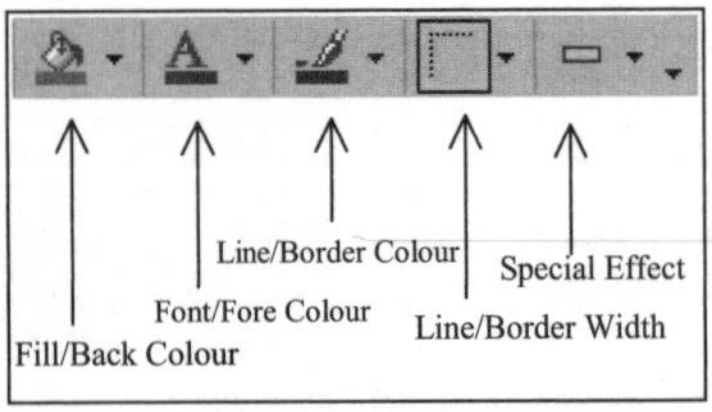

Fig. 8.13 The Form/Report Toolbar Buttons

To use most of these buttons, you simply click the control (in Design view) that contains the feature you want to change and then click the button and make any selections you want.

Do try and experiment with moving and sizing label and data boxes and also increasing their font size. If you don't like the result, simply don't save it. Skills gained here will be used in the Report design section later on.

The Toolbox

The Toolbox can be used either to design a Form or Report from scratch (a task beyond the scope of this book), or to add controls to them, such as a Combo (drop-down) box. The functions of the default tools on the Toolbox are listed in Fig. 8.14 below and described on the following pages. Depending on what you have been doing with the program and what databases you have opened, Access may also show other controls on the Toolbox.

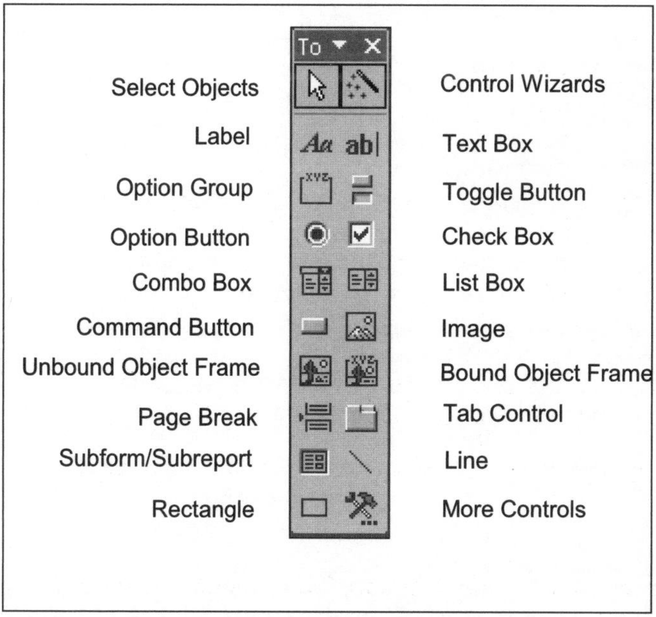

Fig. 8.14 The Default Toolbox Controls

Label

You use labels on a form, report, or data access page to display text such as titles or captions. Labels do not display values from fields, are always unbound (see below) and they stay the same between records.

When you create a label by using the Label tool, the label stands on its own and is not attached to any other control. When you create say a text box, it is automatically given an attached label that displays a caption for that text box. This label appears as a column heading in the Datasheet view of a form, whereas stand-alone labels don't appear in Datasheet view.

Text Box

Text boxes are used to display data from a record on a form, report, or a data access page. They are then said to be bound as they are directly linked to the field data.

Text boxes can also be unbound, or not linked to field data, say to display the results of a calculation or to accept input.

Toggle Button

A toggle button on a form is used to change the state of a field, for example to display a Yes/No, True/False, or On/Off value from an underlying record source. When you click a toggle button that is, say, bound to a Yes/No field in a database, the value in the underlying table displays according to the field's Yes/No property. You can use pictures on toggle buttons, with one picture representing one state of the field, and another when it is 'switched off'.

Toggle buttons are most used in option groups with other buttons.

Option Group

In a form or report, an option group consists of a group frame with a set of check boxes, option buttons, or toggle buttons. It is used to display a limited set of alternatives where only one can be selected at a time. An option group makes selecting a value easy because you can just click the value that you want.

Option Button

You can use option buttons in three main ways:

- as a stand-alone control to display a Yes/No value from an underlying record source,
- in an option group to display values to choose from,
- in a custom dialogue box to accept user input.

With the first two uses the option buttons would be bound, and in the last unbound.

Check Box

You can use a check box on a form, report, or data access page as a stand-alone control to display a Yes/No value from an underlying table, query, or SQL statement. If the box contains a check mark, the value is Yes; if it doesn't, the value is No.

List Box

It is often quicker and easier to select a value from a list than to remember it and then type it into a form field. A list box gives this facility, and providing a fixed list of choices also helps prevent simple typing errors. In a form, a list box can have one or more columns. If a multiple-column list box is bound, Access stores the values from one of the columns.

Combo Box

A combo box is like a text box and a list box combined. When you enter text or select a value in a bound combo box the entered or selected value is inserted into the field that the combo box is bound to.

On a form, you can use a combo box instead of a list box; it takes up less room, and you can type new values in it, as well as select values from a list.

Command Button

You use a command button on a form or data access page to start a macro to implement an action or a set of actions. The macro, or event procedure, must be attached to the button's OnClick property. You can create over thirty different types of command buttons with the Command Button Wizard.

Image

The image control is used to add unbound images, or pictures, to a form, as long as you will not need to edit them in the future. The images are stored in the database itself, which makes them very fast to load.

Unbound Object Frame

Unbound object frames can be used to add unbound images (or other objects like spreadsheet tables) to a frame or report when you may want to be able to edit them directly from the form or report. Double-clicking the image will then open the application that was used to create it so that you can edit it in-situ. The image is slower to load than with Image controls though.

Bound Object Frame

These are similar to the above but are used to display bound OLE objects (images or spreadsheet tables for example) that are actually stored in a table in the database. Double-clicking the object will then open the application that was used to create it so that you can edit it in-situ.

Tab Control

This can be used to present several pages of information as a single set on a form. Each page is given a headed tab and it is accessed by clicking on this tab.

Page Break

The Page Break tool lets you design multiple screen (or page) forms. Remember to place page breaks above, or below, other controls to avoid splitting their data.

Subform / Subreport

A subform is a form within a form and a subreport is a report within a report, the primary form or report being the main one, and the other the 'sub' one. These are especially effective when you want to show data from tables or queries with a one-to-many relationship, as we have seen in our example a few pages back.

Line

Draws a line on a form, report, or data access page. Click anywhere on the form, report, or data access page to create a default-sized line. You can then click and drag it to create a line the size you want.

To make small adjustments to the length or angle of a line, select it, hold down the <Shift> key, and press one of the arrow keys. To make small adjustments in the placement of a line, hold down the <Ctrl> key and press one of the arrow keys. To change the thickness of a line, click the line, and click the arrow next to the Line/ Border Width button on the toolbar and then click the line thickness you want. To change the line style to dots, dashes, etc., right-click the line, select **Properties** from the shortcut menu to open the Property sheet, and then click a border style in the BorderStyle property box, as shown here in Fig. 8.15.

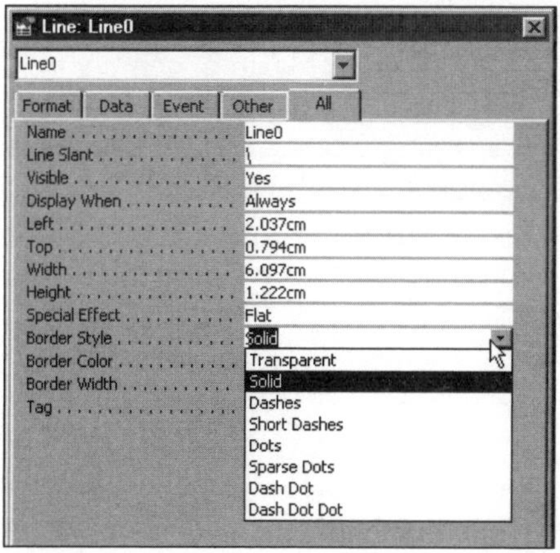

Fig. 8.15 The Property Sheet for a Line

Rectangle

Draws an 'empty' rectangle on a form, report, or data access page. You can change the size, colour and line thickness, etc., by editing the rectangle properties.

More Controls

On our PC this button opens a list of several hundred other control types to use. Many of these require extra software to be installed, but it is well worth experimenting here. The Calendar Control 10.0, for example worked with us, as shown below.

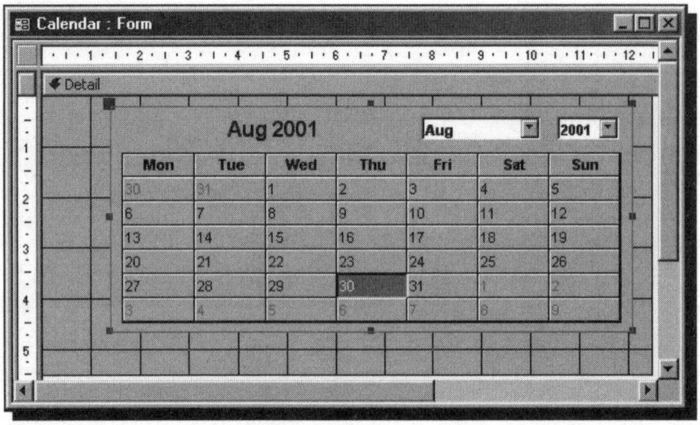

Fig. 8.16 A Calendar Control on a Blank Form

A calendar to be placed on any form in your database will surely have its uses, but you will have to experiment on your own to find them.

We have played around with our Customer Invoice Details form in Design view, as can be seen in Fig. 8.17 at the top of the next page. You should not have too much trouble now with most of the changes. The title is formatted text inside a new Label control and several of the Text Boxes have been re-sized and moved, or even deleted! If you are interested, the vertical bar at the left of the form was removed by setting the 'Record Select' Form Property to No.

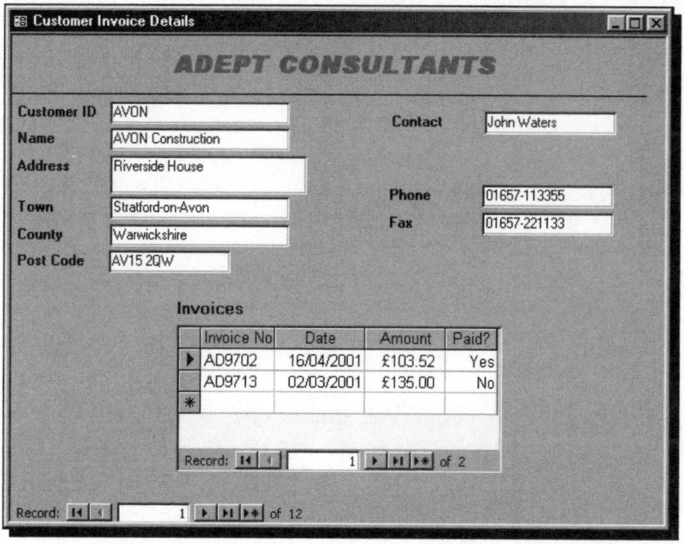

Fig. 8.17 Our Customer Invoices Form Ready For Use

Adding a Combo Box

As an example of using the Toolbox in a form, we will step through the procedure of replacing the CustomerID text box field with a combo box, so that we can select from a drop-down menu when using this field. We will do this in a new form based on the Invoices table of the **Adept 1** database. You should have no trouble by now creating this form (as shown below) with the Form Wizard. Include all the table fields in it, and give it the name Add Invoices.

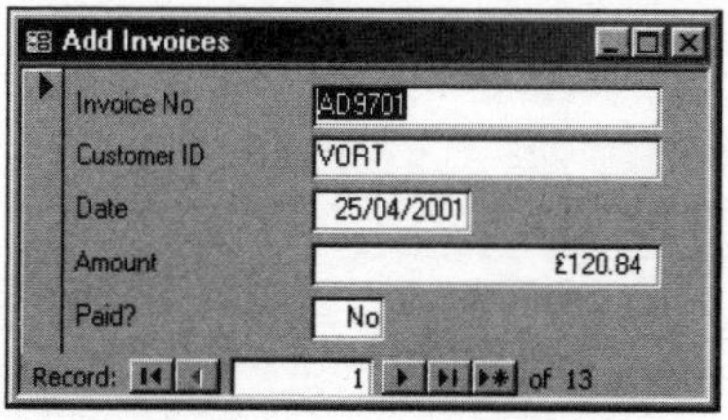

Fig. 8.18 The Add Invoices Form Created with the Form Wizard

With this new Add Invoices form open in Design view, click the CustomerID field, and delete both its Label and Data boxes by clicking each individually and pressing the <Del> key.

Click the Combo Box control on the Toolbox, and point and click at the area where the CustomerID field used to be on the form. In the subsequent Wizard dialogue boxes, select options which will cause the Combo Box to look up the values from the Customers table, and from the CustomerID field and store a selected value in the CustomerID field. Specify that the Combo Box should have the label Customer ID.

Move and size both the Label and Data boxes of the Combo box into the positions shown below.

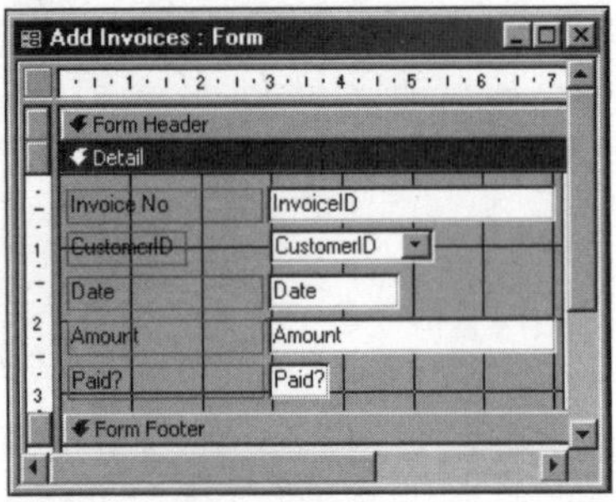

Fig. 8.19 Form in Design View

Click the **Form View** button on the toolbar, followed by the **New Record** button shown here. The entry form should now look like ours in Fig. 8.20 below.

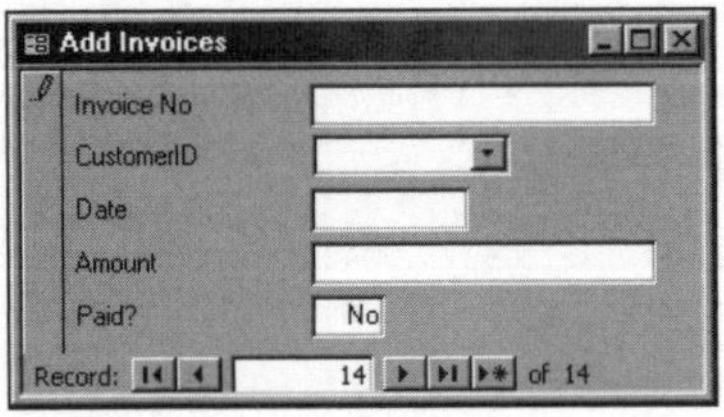

Fig. 8.20 Form Ready for Use

From now on, whenever you want to add a new invoice to the Invoices table, you can open this new form, then click the **New Record** button on either the toolbar or the form itself to

display an empty form. Next, click the down arrow in the Customer ID field to display the drop-down menu shown here. Select one of the existing customers on the list, and click the **Next Record** button at the bottom of the Add Invoices form.

Try the above procedure with the following details:

AD9714 WEST 17/10/01 £140

then verify that indeed the information has been recorded by double-clicking the Invoices table on the Database window.

If you have any problems getting the Combo box to enter data, you may need to check the Join Properties of your database tables, as outlined on page 98. Both the Invoices and Orders tables should be linked with 'type 2' joins.

Changing Controls

With Access 2002, there is another way of replacing a Data box with a Combo box. With the Data box selected, use the **Format**, **Change To**, **Combo Box** menu command and the change will be made straight away. This is very much quicker, but to make the Combo box work you have to put a fairly difficult expression (see page 145 for more) in the Row Source property of the Combo box, as shown in Fig. 8.21 below. To open this Properties box, right click on the Combo box itself and select **Properties** from the shortcut menu.

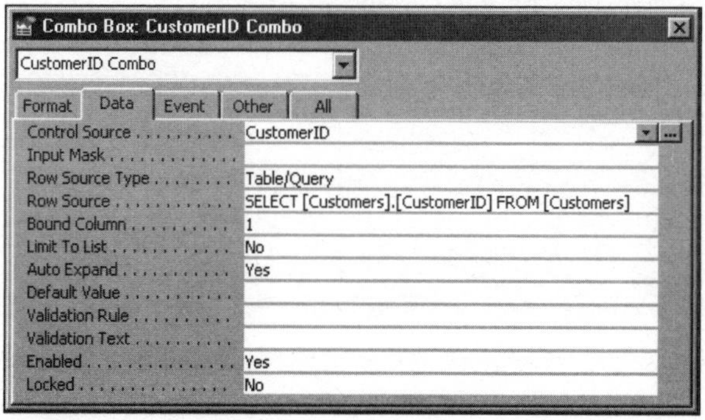

Fig. 8.21 The Data Properties of Our Combo Control

Creating a Database Menu

The sample databases provided with Access 2002 have a starting menu system, known as a Switchboard. If you create a new database with the Database Wizard it creates a switchboard (see Fig. 3.6) that makes it easy to navigate between the forms and reports in the new database. We shall see how to create such a switchboard from scratch, like ours below.

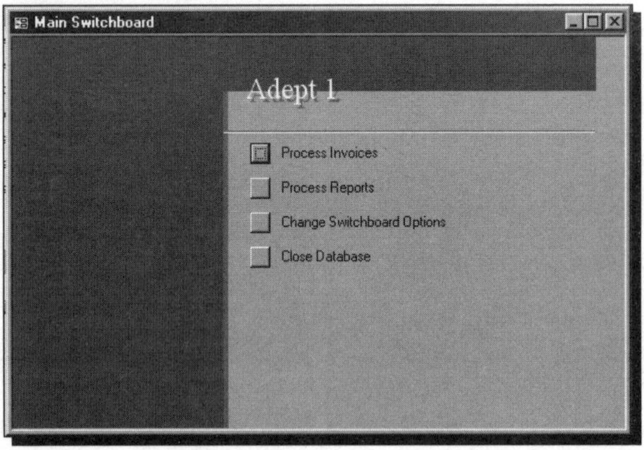

Fig. 8.22 A Database Switchboard, or Menu, System

The Switchboard Manager

To start this procedure, action the **Tools**, **Database Utilities**, **Switchboard Manager** command from the main Access menu, which when used for the first time opens the following message box.

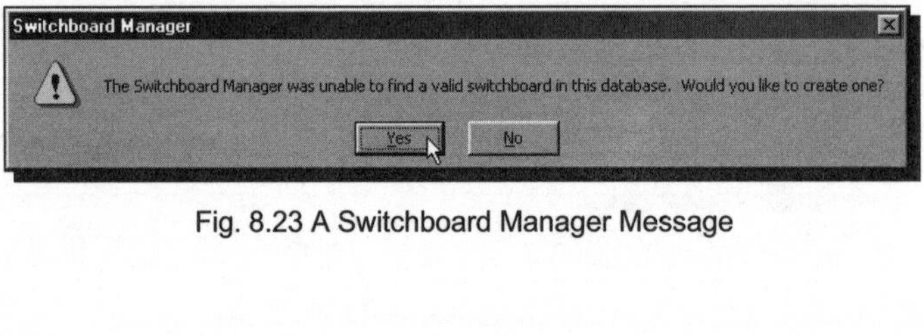

Fig. 8.23 A Switchboard Manager Message

When you select **Yes** a new form, with the name of Switchboard, is placed in the Database window and the Switchboard Manager dialogue box shown in Fig. 8.24 is opened.

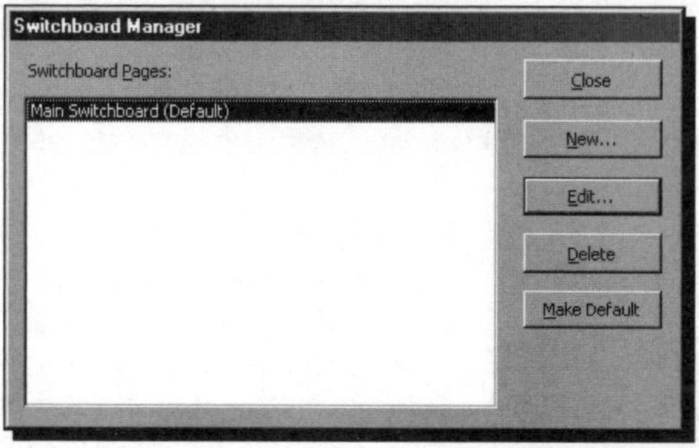

Fig. 8.24 The Switchboard Manager Dialogue Box

In the Switchboard Manager dialogue box, click **New**, type 'Invoices', and click the **OK** button to create a new menu, or switchboard, page of that name. Repeat the process and create another Reports page, as we show in Fig. 8.25.

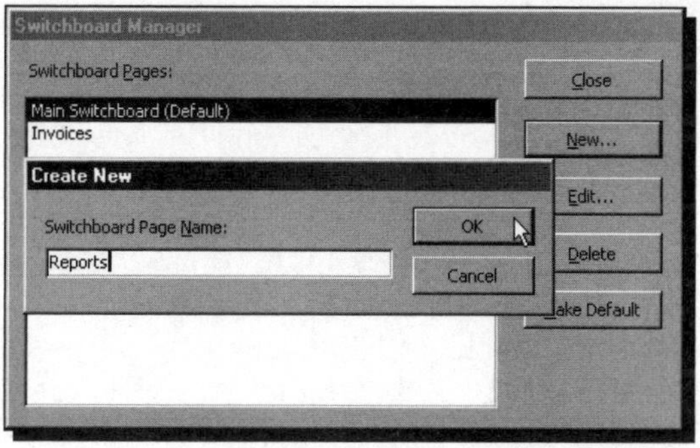

Fig. 8.25 Creating a New Reports Menu Page

You now have three menu pages with nothing on any of them, select the page Main Switchboard and click the **Edit** and **New** buttons in turn. Complete the Edit Switchboard Item box as shown in Fig. 8.26, where **Text** is what will appear on the menu line, **Command** is the action that will be taken and the last line holds any parameters needed.

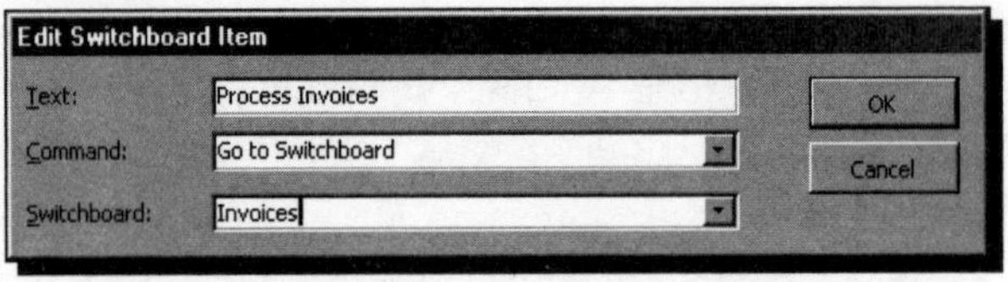

Fig. 8.26 The Edit Switchboard Item Box

You don't actually have to remember anything, where there are options you can click on the down-arrow to select from them.

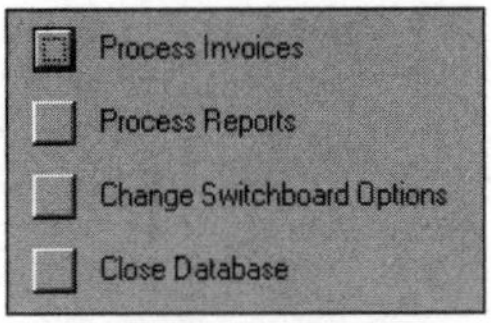

Fig. 8.27 The Main Menu Options

As shown in Fig. 8.27, the next menu item is Process Reports which points to the Reports switchboard page. The Change Switchboard Options item opens the Switchboard Manager with the Design Application **Command**. The last item on the main switchboard is self explanatory and uses the Exit Application **Command** to close the database.

That completes the main page, so click **Close** to return to the Switchboard Manager dialogue box, select the Invoices page and click the **Edit** button. This page has three items, as shown in Fig. 8.28, each one being added by clicking the **New** button. The first one uses the Open Form in Add Mode **Command** to open the Add Invoices form. The second one uses the Open Form in Edit Mode **Command** to open the Customer Invoice Details form, and the last line uses the Go to Switchboard **Command** to return to the Main Switchboard.

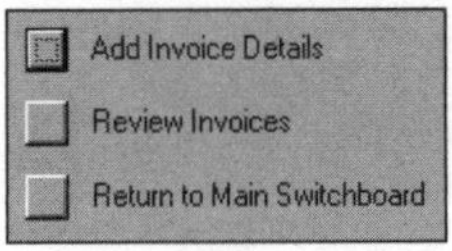

Fig. 8.28 The Invoice Menu Options

At this stage you can place a Return to Main Switchboard item on the Reports page, so that it does not form a dead end. You can finish this menu page yourself after the next chapter.

Pressing **Close** twice should return you to the Database window, where you can finally try out your menu system by double-clicking the Switchboard form entry. Hopefully all will be well and your menu will look something like ours shown on page 130.

You can, of course, customise this form in Design view, but we suggest you go very carefully here. It is easy to corrupt the menu controls. A good idea is to make a copy of the form and play with that until you are happy. Whatever you do, please don't delete the Switchboard form from the Database window. We did this and it was not easy to create another one. Be warned.

To make sure the correct switchboard page opens on your menu, ensure that the word (Default) appears at the end of the Main Switchboard name in the Switchboard Manager dialogue box, if not, then select it and click the **Make Default** button.

An Autostart Menu

If you want your menu system to be displayed whenever you open the database, make the changes shown in Fig. 8.29 below, in the Startup dialogue box. This is opened with the **Tools**, **Startup** menu command.

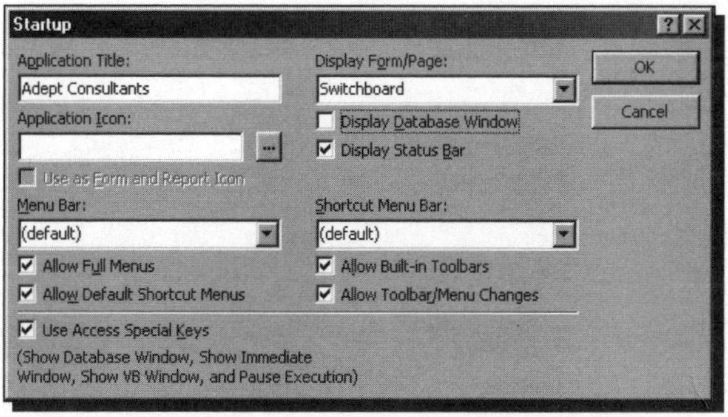

Fig. 8.29 The Database Startup Dialogue Box

If the **Display Database Window** check box is not selected the Database window will not automatically open with the database. With this setting, if you need it, you will then have to press the **F11** key.

Take care with some of the options in the Startup box. You should only make changes to the four lower check boxes when your database design is finalised and you have made a backup copy of it. For example, if you deselect the **Allow Full Menus** option, you will no longer be able to access Design view from your database!

Good luck with your menu system. Ours is obviously fairly simplistic and is for example only. You can make yours as complex as your own databases require.

9

Using Reports

In Access, a report is an effective way to present data in printed format. The data in a report is taken from a database table, query, or SQL statement, and the other report information is stored in the report's design. This is shown graphically in Fig. 9.1 below, which was part of an Access Help page.

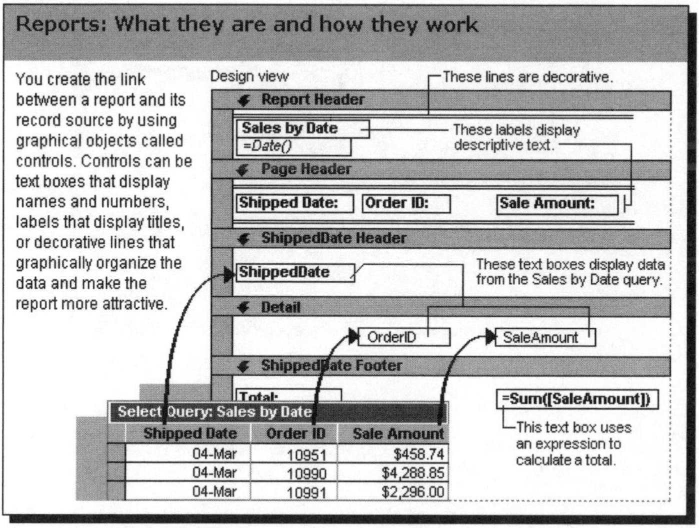

Fig. 9.1 Some Help Information on Access Reports

When designing a report you can combine data from any of the tables, or queries, of your database. As with a form, you do this in Design view by adding controls to the design grid. These controls define the source of the information in the database, and its printed appearance.

The Report Wizard

To see how easy it can be, we will use the skills gained in manipulating Access forms in Design view to produce a very quick, but acceptable, report using the Report Wizard. In our example database, **Adept 1**, we will produce a report based on the Unpaid Invoices query.

Click the Reports tab on the Database window and then press the **New** button, to open the New Report dialogue box as shown in Fig. 9.2 below.

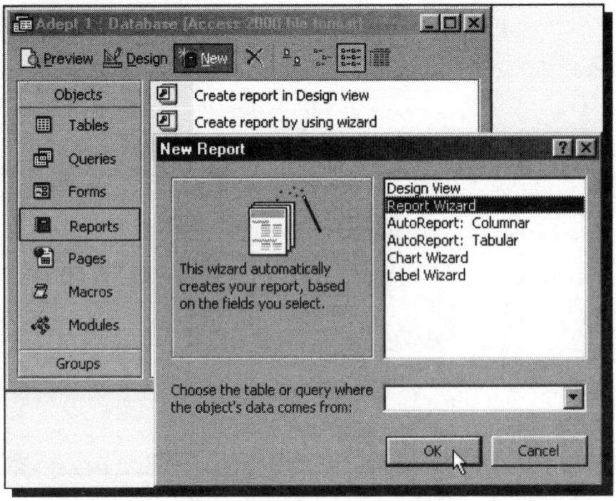

Fig. 9.2 Selecting the Report Wizard from the New Report Box

Select the Report Wizard option, and choose Unpaid Invoices as the query where the report data will come from, and press OK.

Select all the fields (except for Paid?) to appear on your report. Select the InvoiceID field as the sort field, accept all other default settings, and give it the name Unpaid Invoices Report.

The report is quickly created for you as shown in Fig. 9.3 on the next page, but the format leaves a lot to be desired. The problem is mainly that all the text fields are left justified while numerical fields are right justified.

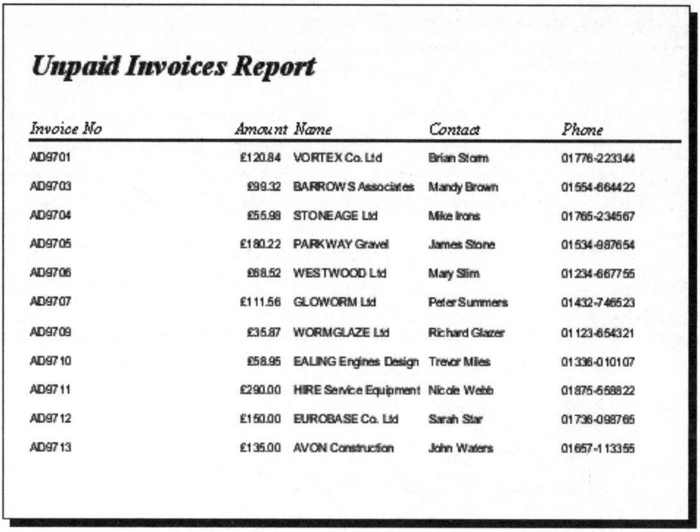

Unpaid Invoices Report

Invoice No	*Amount*	*Name*	*Contact*	*Phone*
AD9701	£120.84	VORTEX Co. Ltd	Brian Storm	01776-223344
AD9703	£99.32	BARROWS Associates	Mandy Brown	01554-664422
AD9704	£55.98	STONEAGE Ltd	Mike Irons	01765-234567
AD9705	£180.22	PARKWAY Gravel	James Stone	01534-987654
AD9706	£68.52	WESTWOOD Ltd	Mary Slim	01234-667755
AD9707	£111.56	GLOWORM Ltd	Peter Summers	01432-746523
AD9709	£35.87	WORMGLAZE Ltd	Richard Glazer	01123-654321
AD9710	£58.95	EALING Engines Design	Trevor Miles	01336-010107
AD9711	£290.00	HIRE Service Equipment	Nicole Webb	01875-558822
AD9712	£150.00	EUROBASE Co. Ltd	Sarah Star	01736-098765
AD9713	£135.00	AVON Construction	John Waters	01657-113355

Fig. 9.3 A Raw Report Created by the Report Wizard

What we need to do is display it in Design view so that we can change the position of the numeric fields. To do this, select the report in the Database window and click the Design icon on the toolbar which displays the underlying format of the report as shown in Fig. 9.4 below:

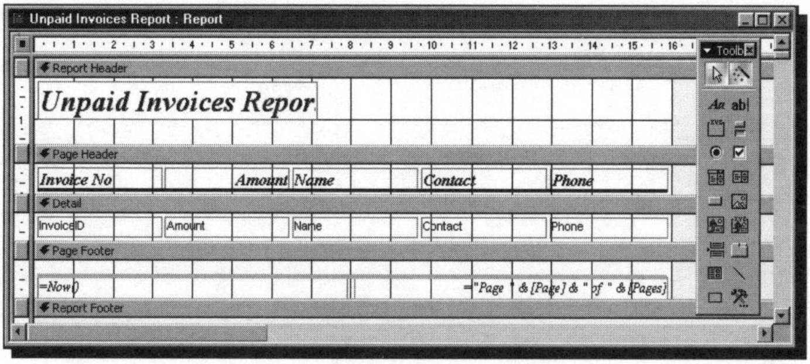

Fig. 9.4 The New Report in Design View

Use the mouse to lengthen the title label, then move the Amount data box to the left, and right justify the text in the Amount label and data boxes and make them smaller, as shown in Fig. 9.5 on the next page.

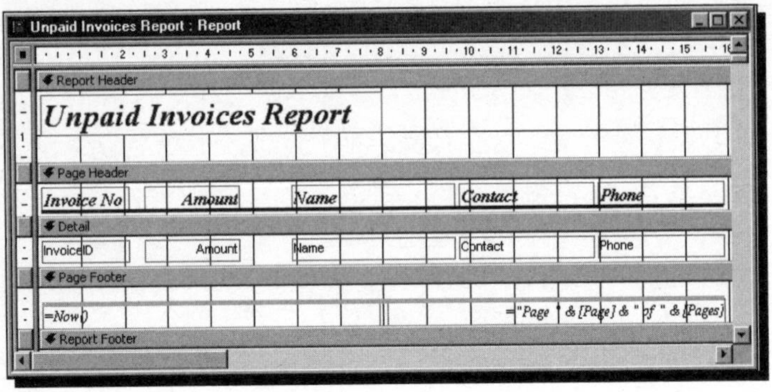

Fig. 9.5 The Modified Report in Design View

The corresponding report now prints as follows:

Unpaid Invoices Report

Invoice No	*Amount*	*Name*	*Contact*	*Phone*
AD9701	£120.84	VORTEX Co. Ltd	Brian Storm	01776-223344
AD9703	£99.32	BARROWS Associates	Mandy Brown	01554-664422
AD9704	£55.98	STONEAGE Ltd	Mike Irons	01765-234567
AD9705	£180.22	PARKWAY Gravel	James Stone	01534-987654
AD9706	£68.52	WESTWOOD Ltd	Mary Slim	01234-667755
AD9707	£111.56	GLOWORM Ltd	Peter Summers	01432-746523
AD9709	£35.87	WORMGLAZE Ltd	Richard Glazer	01123-654321
AD9710	£58.95	EALING Engines Design	Trevor Miles	01336-010107
AD9711	£290.00	HIRE Service Equipment	Nicole Webb	01875-558822
AD9712	£150.00	EUROBASE Co. Ltd	Sarah Star	01736-098765
AD9713	£135.00	AVON Construction	John Waters	01657-113355

Fig. 9.6 The Modified Report Print Out

This layout is obviously far more acceptable than that of the original report created by the Report Wizard. It does not take much tweaking to get good results, and of course you only need to do this once, as long as you save your changes. The next time you double-click the name of this report in the Database window, it will be produced again with the most up-to-date data.

Types of Access Reports

In Design view you can, if you have the skill and time, create reports completely on your own. Initially we are sure most people will be happy using one of the following Wizards to create their reports, and then spend a few minutes (hopefully not hours) getting the final result.

Report Wizard - Automatically creates reports based on fields and options you select.

Autoreport: Columnar - Automatically produces a columnar report.

Autoreport: Tabular - Automatically produces a tabular report.

Chart Wizard - creates a report with a chart.

Label Wizard - creates a report formatted for you to print on mailing labels.

With the AutoReport options above, you select one record source, such as a table or query and the Wizard then uses all the fields from that source and applies the last autoformat you used to the report. With the Chart Wizard, however, you can select fields from more than one table or query source.

Report Views

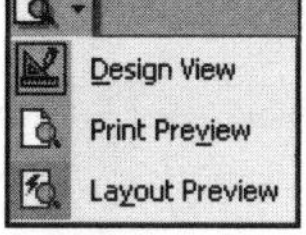

Fig. 9.7
Report Views

With Access 2002 there are three possible screen views of a report accessed by clicking the down-arrow next to the **View** toolbar button, shown here. **Print Preview** shows the report on the screen as it will be printed with all its data. In **Design View** you change the layout and content of a report. **Layout Preview** is only available from Design view, and shows the report layout with only a small sample of data.

Help on Report Building

The reporting section of Access 2002 is very powerful and we only have space to give a flavour of it here. We suggest you spend several hours at least in the Help section, accessed as usual with the **F1** key.

Fig. 9.8 The Access Help Contents Pane on Reports

Some of the sections are graphical, very detailed and very easy to understand, as in the example shown here.

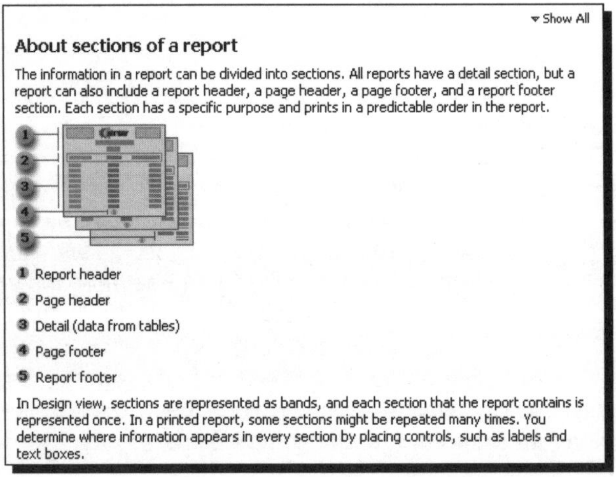

Fig. 9.9 A Sample of Access Help Detail on Reports

The Northwind Database

The other main source of inspiration on reports, and other database components, is the Northwind sample database packaged with Access and introduced here on page 44.

Open this database and have a look through the reports that are in it (14 in our case, but you may have a different version). We have printed out a 'cut down' sample from the Employee Sales by Country report in Fig. 9.10 below, and show it in Design view in Fig. 9.11 on the next page, so that you can compare them and get some idea how the final report is made up.

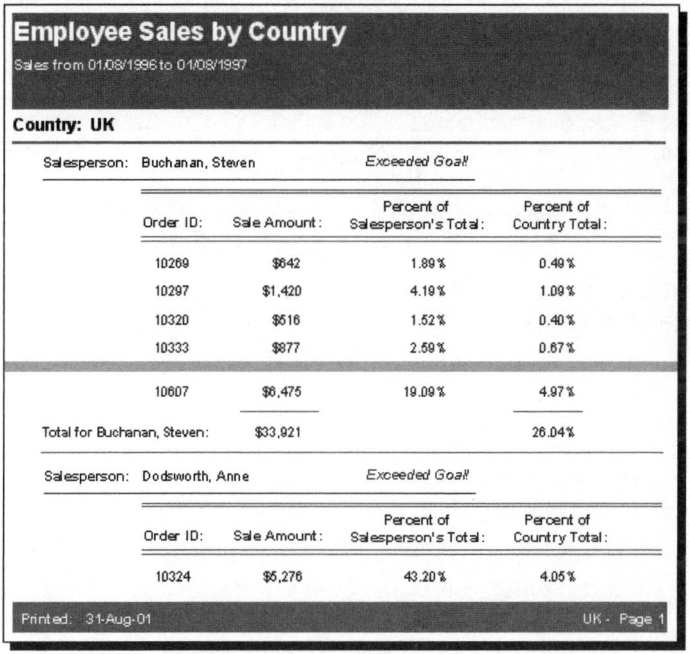

Employee Sales by Country

Sales from 01/08/1996 to 01/08/1997

Country: UK

Salesperson: Buchanan, Steven *Exceeded Goal!*

Order ID:	Sale Amount:	Percent of Salesperson's Total:	Percent of Country Total:
10269	$642	1.89%	0.49%
10297	$1,420	4.19%	1.09%
10320	$516	1.52%	0.40%
10333	$877	2.59%	0.67%
10607	$6,475	19.09%	4.97%

Total for Buchanan, Steven: $33,921 26.04%

Salesperson: Dodsworth, Anne *Exceeded Goal!*

Order ID:	Sale Amount:	Percent of Salesperson's Total:	Percent of Country Total:
10324	$5,276	43.20%	4.05%

Printed: 31-Aug-01 UK - Page 1

Fig. 9.10 A Report from the Northwind Sample Database

The data is a little dated, but it is the design we are looking at! The report has two grouping selections, the first based on the Country, and the second giving details of the sales persons in that country.

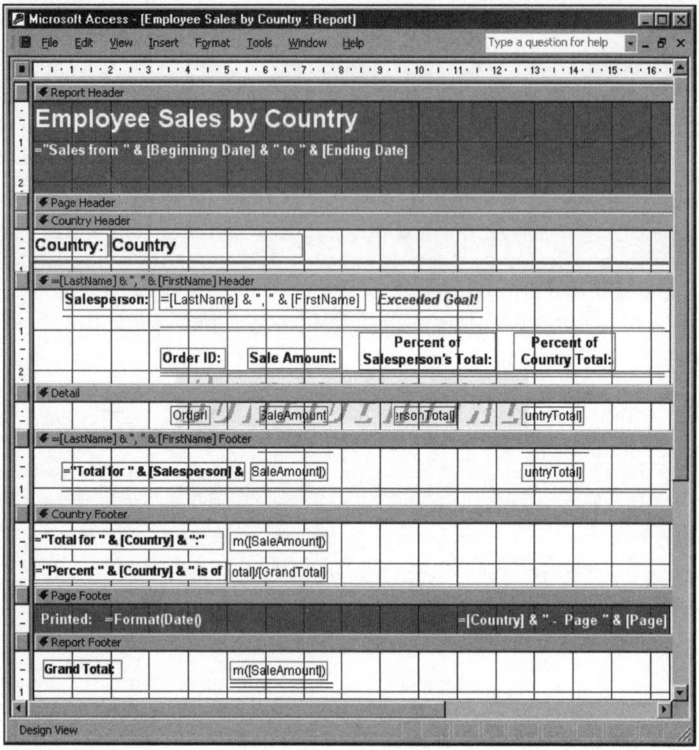

Fig. 9.11 The Same Northwind Report in Design View

There are nine bands shown above in this report and what prints in each band of the final report depends on the controls (mainly Labels and Text Boxes) placed on it. The function of each band and where its output appears is shown below:

Report Header - appears at the start of a report
Page Header - appears at the top of each report page
Group 1 Header - appears above a new group
Group 2 Header - appears above a new group
Report Detail - the main body of report data
Group 2 Footer - appears at the end of a group
Group 1 Footer - appears at the end of a group
Page Footer - appears at the bottom of each page
Report Footer - appears at the end of a report.

Sorting and Grouping Records

In the previous example there were two report groups, but you can sort and group on up to 10 fields or expressions in a

report. You control this with the report open in Design view, by clicking the **Sorting And Grouping** button on the toolbar to open the Sorting And Grouping dialogue box, shown below.

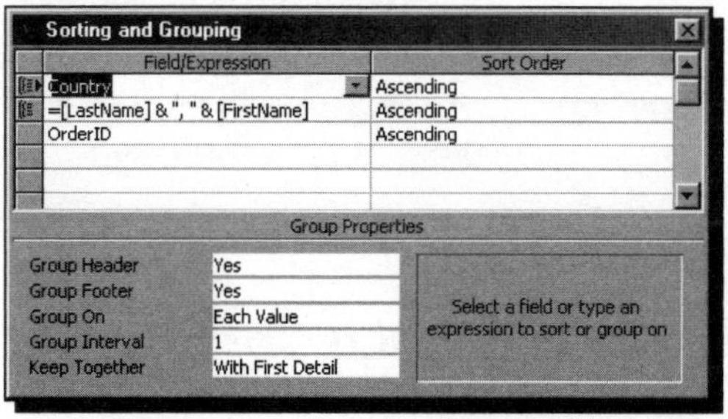

Fig. 9.12 The Sorting and Grouping Dialogue Box

Sorting Records

In the first row of the **Field/Expression** column, select a field name from the drop-down list, or type an expression. The field or expression in this first row is the first sorting level. The second row is the second sorting level, etc. By default Access sets the **Sort Order** to Ascending which sorts from A to Z or 0 to 9. To change the sort order, select Descending from the Sort Order drop-down list.

Grouping Records

In the Sorting And Grouping dialogue box, click the field whose group properties you want to set. You must set either Group Header or Group Footer to Yes in order to create a group level and set the other grouping properties.

Group Header Adds or removes a group header for the field or expression.

Group Footer	Adds or removes a group footer for the field or expression.
Group On	Specifies how you want the values grouped. The options depend on the data type of the field. If you group on an expression, all the data type options become available.
Group Interval	Specifies any interval that is valid for the values in the field or expression you are grouping on.
Keep Together	Specifies whether all or only part of a group is printed on the same page.

Creating a Calculated Control

It is often very useful to have a report calculate values from the data extracted from the database, such as totals, averages, percentages, etc. To describe how to do this, we will place a total value on the Unpaid Invoices Report we designed at the beginning of the chapter.

Open the Unpaid Invoices Report of the **Adept 1** database in Design view as usual and drag the Report Footer down to make room for the new controls. Select the grey line in the Page Footer band, by clicking it, and copy and paste it into the new space. Click the Text Box tool in the toolbox and 'drag' a new box about the same size as and below the Amount control in the Detail band, as shown in Fig. 9.13.

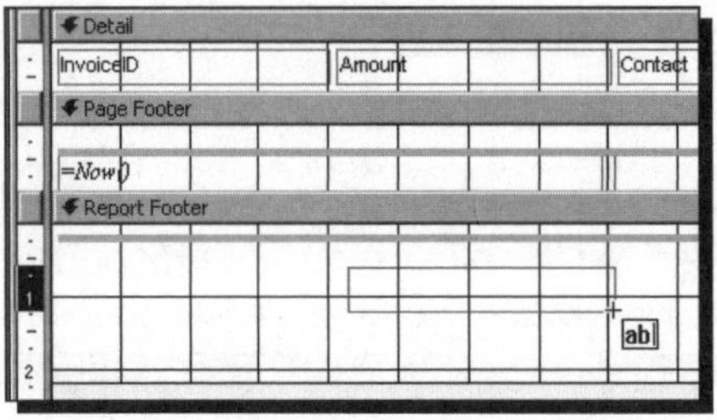

Fig. 9.13 Placing a Text Box Control in a Report

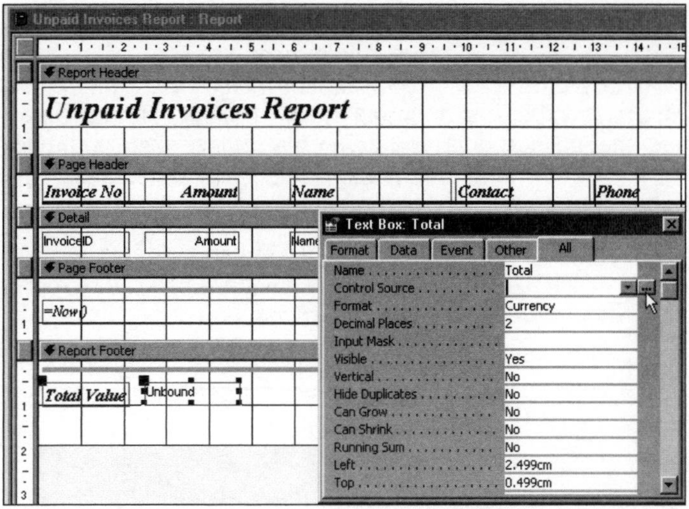

Fig. 9.14 Setting the Text Box Control Source Property

Type 'Total Value' in the Label that is placed to the left of the Text Box, and re-size the boxes as shown above.

We must now enter the Expression into the Text box to carry out the required calculation. Make sure the Text Box control is selected, click the **Properties** button on the toolbar to display the control's property sheet, and click the **All** tab, as shown in Fig. 9.14. Type the new control name 'Total' in the Name property box and click the Build button next to the Control-Source property box. This opens the Expression Builder, shown in Fig. 9.15.

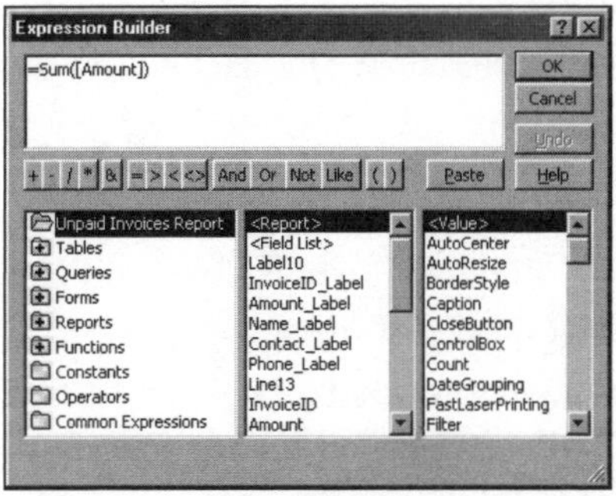

Fig. 9.15 The Expression Builder

In fact with a text box, you can type the expression directly into it, but we wanted to introduce the Expression Builder! Click **Help** to read about this feature.

The expression you need to total the Amount field is:

```
=Sum([amount])
```

Either type this into the Expression Builder, or experiment with the builder until you have this expression in the top

window, and then press **OK** to place the expression in the properties sheet. Clicking the **Print Preview** toolbar button should now show the following result.

Unpaid Invoices Report

Invoice No	*Amount*	*Name*	*Contact*	*Phone*
AD9701	£120.84	VORTEX Co. Ltd	Brian Storm	01776-223344
AD9703	£99.32	BARROWS Associates	Mandy Brown	01554-664422
AD9704	£55.98	STONEAGE Ltd	Mike Irons	01765-234567
AD9705	£180.22	PARKWAY Gravel	James Stone	01534-987654
AD9706	£68.52	WESTWOOD Ltd	Mary Slim	01234-667755
AD9707	£111.56	GLOWORM Ltd	Peter Summers	01432-746523
AD9709	£35.87	WORMGLAZE Ltd	Richard Glazer	01123-654321
AD9710	£58.95	EALING Engines Design	Trevor Miles	01336-010107
AD9711	£290.00	HIRE Service Equipment	Nicole Webb	01875-558822
AD9712	£150.00	EUROBASE Co. Ltd	Sarah Star	01736-098765
AD9713	£135.00	AVON Construction	John Waters	01657-113355
Total Value	£1,306.26			

Fig. 9.16 Print Preview of the Modified Report

In a calculated control you should always start each expression with the = operator as can be seen on the next page where we list the other arithmetic expressions you can use in an Access database report or form.

It is usually easier to type the expression straight into a text box, or a property box, and don't forget that if you need more room to type the expression in the box, the <Shift+**F2**> keystroke combination will open the Zoom box for you.

Arithmetic Expressions

Expression	*Description*
=Avg([Field])	Uses the Avg function to display the average of the values of the 'Field' control.
=Count([Field])	Uses the Count function to display the number of records in the 'Field' control.
=Sum([Field])	Uses the Sum function to display the sum of the values of the 'Field' control.
=Sum([Field1]*[Field2])	Uses the Sum function to display the sum of the product of the values of the 'Field1' and 'Field2' controls.
=[Sales]/Sum([Sales])	Displays the percentage of sales, determined by dividing the value of the Sales control by the sum of all the values of the Sales control. The control's Format property must be set to Percent for this to work.

Access has quite an extensive list of expressions that can be used in tables and forms. Amongst other things, these can be used to handle text, numbers, dates, page numbers and control values.

To find out more on these, type 'expressions' in the **Ask a Question** box (on the Access menu bar), press the <Enter> key and select the 'About expressions' topic from the list produced. This will open the Help system at the correct place for you.

All that remains to be done now is to add a menu item to the Reports page of the Switchboard form. We will leave that for you to do. In a real database it would be useful to have every report listed on this menu page.

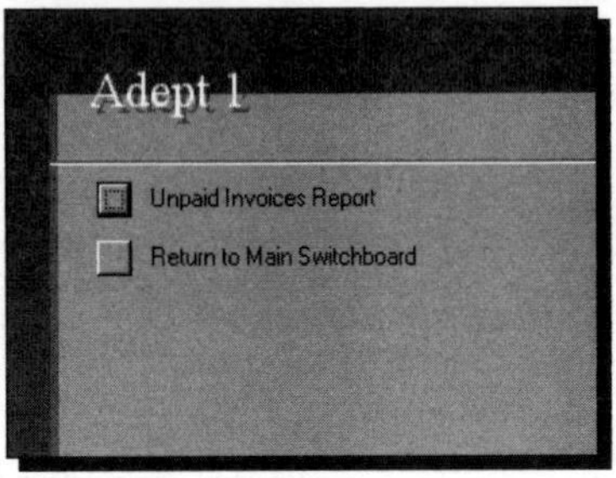

Fig. 9.17 The 'Process Reports' Switchboard Page

Printing a Report

Printing a report to paper in Access is just the same as printing from any other Microsoft Windows application. If necessary, first use the **File**, **Page Setup** command to set the paper size, source, orientation and margin settings. With

the report either open or selected in the Database window, click the **Print** toolbar button to use the current printer settings.

If you want to change the printer settings, you should use the **File**, **Print** command, or <Ctrl+P>, to open the Print dialogue box (shown in Fig. 4.34 on page 67), make the changes you want, and then click the **OK** button to start the printing operation.

10

Working with Data

In this chapter we discuss several aspects of working with data; masking, importing, linking and embedding. The first is useful for restricting data input into an Access field, such as a postcode or a telephone number, to a given data mask so as to eliminate input errors.

The Input Mask Property

You can use the Input Mask property to make data entry easier and control the values you enter in a text box. For example, you could create an input mask for a Post Code field that shows you exactly how to enter a new postcode.

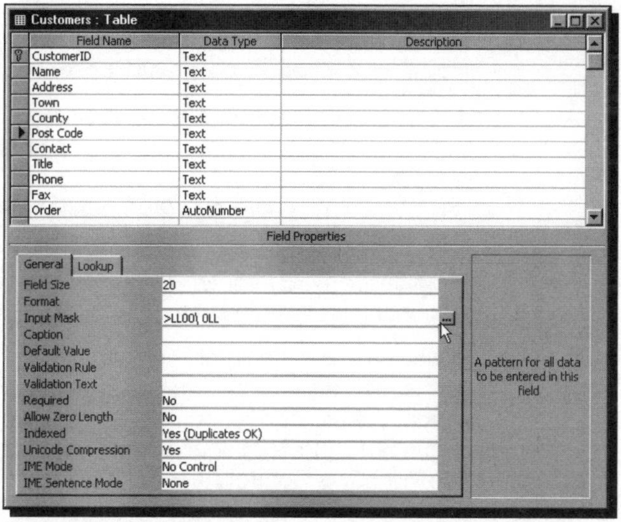

Fig. 10.1 The Default Input Mask for the Post Code Field

To see an input mask, open the **Adept 1** database, select the Customers table, press the **Design View** button, and select the Post Code field. The input mask appears in the Field Properties box, shown in Fig. 10.1 on the previous page.

The Input Mask property can contain up to three sections separated by semicolons (;). Within each section a certain number of characters are allowed. These characters and their description are listed below.

Character	***Description***
0	Signifies a digit (0 to 9); entry required. The plus (+) and minus (–) signs are not allowed.
9	Signifies a digit or space; entry not required. The plus and minus signs are not allowed.
#	Signifies a digit or space; entry not required, spaces are displayed as blanks while in Edit mode, but blanks are removed when data is saved. The plus and minus signs are allowed.
L	Signifies a letter (A to Z); entry required.
?	Signifies a letter (A to Z); entry optional.
A	Signifies a letter or digit; entry required.
a	Signifies a letter or digit; entry optional.
&	Signifies any character or a space; entry required.
C	Signifies any character or a space; entry optional.
. , : ; - /	Signifies a decimal placeholder and thousand, date, and time separators. (The actual character used depends on the settings in the Regional Settings section of the Windows Control Panel).
<	Causes all characters to be converted to lowercase.

>	Causes all characters to be converted to uppercase.
!	Causes the input mask to display from right to left, rather than from left to right, when characters on the left side of the input mask are optional. Characters typed into the mask always fill it from left to right. You can include the exclamation point anywhere in the input mask.
\	Causes the character that follows to be displayed as the literal character (for example, \A is displayed as just A).

Thus, we can interpret the postcode mask shown in Fig. 10.1 as follows:

> Convert all characters entered to upper case.
L Letter (A-Z) expected; entry required.
L Letter (A-Z) expected; entry required.
0 Digit (0-9) expected; entry required.
0 Digit (0-9) expected; entry required.
**** Cause character following backslash (in this case a space) to appear as such
0 Digit (0-9) expected; entry required.
L Letter (A-Z) expected; entry required.
L Letter (A-Z) expected; entry required.

However, this postcode (two letters followed by two numbers, then a space followed by one number, then two letters, will not be adequate for all postcode variations encountered in the UK.

For example, some codes have only one number following the first two letters, like CB1 2PU, others particularly in London have only one leading letter, like N1 0RD, while if you write to the BBC you will need the W1A 1AA code.

A postcode mask suitable for most eventualities in the UK could be:

>LAaaaaaa

To experiment with input masks, place the insertion pointer in the Post Code field of the Customers table. This causes a dotted button ... to appear at the extreme right of the field which, when clicked, activates the Input Mask Wizard, as shown in Fig. 10.2 below.

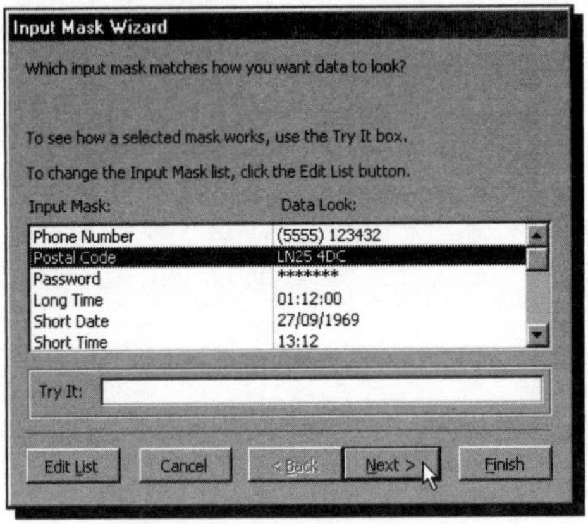

Fig. 10.2 The Input Mask Wizard

Select the Post Code from the Input Mask list, and press **Next** to display the second dialogue box (Fig. 10.3) in which you can edit the default Input Mask. You can also type the variations of the postcode in the Try It box.

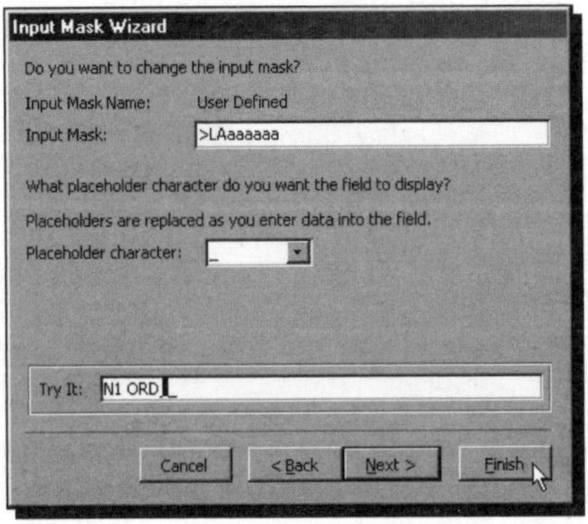

Fig. 10.3 Changing an Input Mask with the Wizard

Note: If you want to create a password-entry control, use the Password input mask to set the Input Mask property to the word 'Password'. This displays an asterisk (*) on the screen for every typed character.

Only characters that you type directly in a control or combo box are affected by the input mask. Microsoft Access ignores any input masks when you import data, or run an action query.

If you define an input mask and also set the Format property for the same field, the Format property takes precedence when the data is displayed. The data in the underlying table itself is not changed, but the Format property affects the way it is displayed.

The three sections of an input mask and their description are listed below.

Section	***Description***
First	Specifies the input mask itself, for example, >LL00\ 0LL or (0000) 000000.
Second	Specifies whether Access stores the literal display characters in the table when you enter data. If you use 0 for this section, all literal display characters (for example, the parentheses in a phone number input mask) are stored with the value; if you enter 1 or leave this section blank, only characters typed into the control are stored.
Third	Specifies the character that Access displays for the space where you should type a character in the input mask. For this section, you can use any character; to display an empty string, use a space enclosed in quotation marks (" ").

The Input Mask Wizard will set the property for you.

Importing or Linking Data

Microsoft Access has an extensive help topic on importing and linking data created in other programs. Below we present the most important parts of this information so as to make it easy for you to follow.

Access can import or link table data from other Access databases (versions 2.0, 7.0/95, 8/97, 9/2000 and 10/2002), as well as data from other programs, such as Excel, dBASE, FoxPro, or Paradox. You can also import or link HTML tables and lists, which can reside on your local PC, a network, or an Internet server.

Importing data creates a copy of the information in a new table in your current Access database; the source table or file is not altered. Linking data allows you to read and update data in the external data source without importing; the external data source's format is not altered so that you can continue to use the file with the program that created it originally, and you can also add, delete, or edit such data using Access.

In general, you import or link information depending on the imposed situation, as follows:

Imposed Situation	***Method to Adopt***
Inserted data needs to be updated in Access as changes are made to the data in the source file, or Source file will always be available and you want to minimise the size of the Access data file.	Link
Inserted information might need to be updated but source file might not be always accessible, or Access data file needs to be edited without having these changes reflected in the source file.	Import

If you have data in any of the following programs or formats, you can either import or link such files.

Data Source	***Version or Format***
Excel spreadsheets	3, 4, 5, 7/95, 8/97, 9/2000, 10/2002
Lotus 1-2-3 spreadsheets	.wks, .wk1, .wk3, & .wk4
dBASE	III, IV, 5, 7 (Linking may require updated drivers)
MS Visual FoxPro	2.x, 3.0, 5.0, 6.x (import)
Paradox	3.x, 4.x, 5.0, 8.0 (Linking may require updated drivers)
MS Exchange	All versions
Delimited text files	All character sets
Fixed-width text files	All character sets
HTML	1.0 (if a list), 2.0, 3.x (if a table or list)
XML Documents	All versions

If you have a program which can export, convert, or save its data in one of these formats, you can import that data as well.

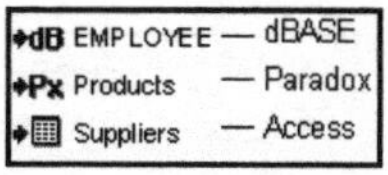

Access uses different icons to represent linked tables and tables that are stored in the current database, as shown here. The icon that represents a linked table remains in the Database window along with tables in the current database, so you can open the table whenever you want.

Access displays a different icon for tables from each type of source database. If you delete the icon for a linked table, you delete the link to the table, but not the external table itself.

When importing data, you cannot append it to existing tables (except when importing spreadsheet or text files). However, once you have imported a table, you can use an append query to add its data to another table.

Linked and Embedded Images

Images can be placed in object frames on Access forms or reports, as shown with one of our forms in Fig. 10.5. In this example the embedded banner image at the top, which displays with every record, was simply pasted into an Image control frame in Design mode.

The main linked image on the form is different for every record so is 'bound' to the underlying table field, and is placed in a Bound Object frame. To enter a new linked image select the field and use the **Insert**, **Object** menu command and select **Create from File** to open the Microsoft Access box, shown in Fig. 10.4. Type in the **File** name, select the **Link** check box, and press **OK**. As long as you don't move the linked source file, the image will show whenever the record is viewed.

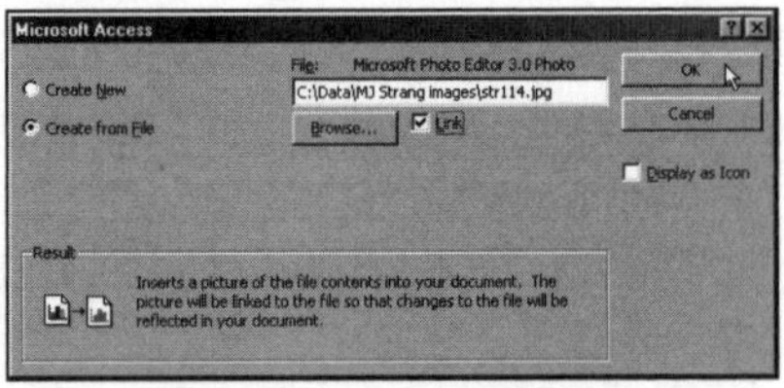

Fig. 10.4 Linking to a File

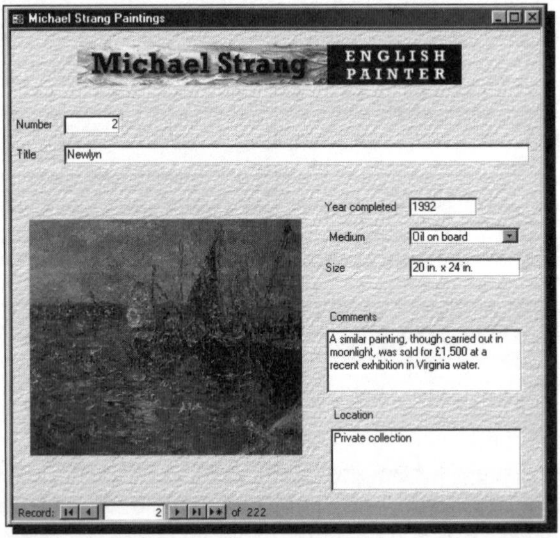

Fig. 10.5 An Access Form with Bound and Unbound Images

11

Access and the Internet

Microsoft has tried to integrate Access 2002 with the Internet and the Web, providing support in several ways:

- Access tables, forms, queries, and reports can contain hypertext links to objects on the Web, or elsewhere.
- You can access the Web from within a database.
- You can save tables, forms, queries, and reports as HTML pages readable by Web browsers.
- You can create 'live' Web pages based on data contained in a database.

The first two of these let you view other Internet files from your database, while the last two makes it possible for your data to be available to the outside world.

Using Hypertext Links

Hypertext links are elements on a Web page that you can click with your mouse, to jump to another Web document. You are actually fetching another file to your PC, and the link is an address that uniquely identifies the location of the target file, wherever it may be. This address is known as a Uniform Resource Locator (URL for short).

Access incorporates hypertext in two ways.

- Through hypertext fields in tables containing links, which you can click to retrieve the linked target.
- Through hyperlinks inserted as elements within forms and reports.

For an Internet link to work you must obviously have access to the Internet from your PC. The targets of these links, however, need not be Internet pages but can be other files on a hard disc drive, or objects within a database.

Creating a Hyperlink Field

To create a Hyperlink field in an open table, select Design view, create the new field, click the Data Type drop-down arrow, and then click Hyperlink. Make sure you save the changes to the table, by clicking the **Save** toolbar button.

Inserting a Hyperlink

You use the **Insert Hyperlink** button to create a hyperlink within a Hyperlink field or as hypertext within a form or report. A hyperlink, in Access, consists of the text that the user sees that describes the link, the URL of the link's target, and a 'ScreenTip' that appears whenever the pointer passes over the link.

Within a Hyperlink field or while editing a form or report in Design view, click the **Insert Hyperlink** button on the toolbar to open the Insert Hyperlink dialogue box, shown in Fig. 11.1 below.

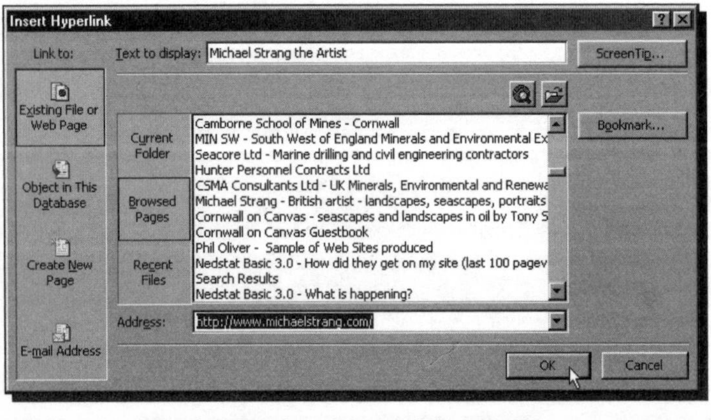

Fig. 11.1 The Insert Hyperlink Dialogue Box

If necessary, click **Existing File or Web Page** on the **Link to** bar and enter the hyperlink text in the **Text to display** box. Specify the linked document by either typing its filename or URL in the **Address** box, or choosing from any of the **Current Folder**, **Browsed Pages** or **Recent Files** lists. Hopefully there won't be too many embarrassing references in these lists, big brother is watching you these days!

Fig. 11.2 A Hyperlink ScreenTip

Click **ScreenTip** to create a ScreenTip that will be displayed whenever the mouse pointer moves over the hyperlink.

Clicking **OK** will place the link onto your Access object. Our example above placed the link on a form shown in Fig. 11.3 below in both Design and Form views.

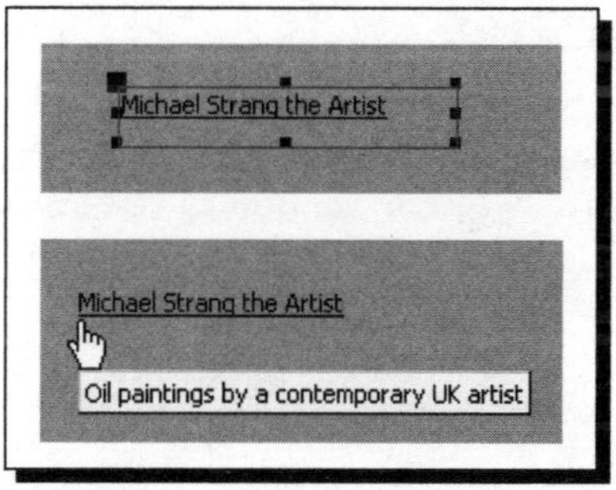

Fig. 11.3 An Example Hyperlink in Design and Form Views

Navigating the Internet from Access

Once you click a hyperlink it is activated and, as long as you are connected to the Internet, Access displays the Web toolbar which contains buttons that help you navigate the Web, as shown in Fig. 11.4 on the next page.

Fig. 11.4 The Access Web Toolbar

In fact, if you are using Explorer 5+ as your browser, its window replaces that of Access while you are viewing a live Web page. As you progress through a series of links, the toolbar displays buttons that allow you to go forward and backward through the sequence. It also includes buttons to access a list of 'favorite' Web pages or a 'start', or Home, page. So far these are all standard browser buttons, the exception being the **Show Only Web Toolbar** button, shown

here, whose very useful toggle function is self explanatory. It gives you more screen space by closing the other Access toolbars.

Creating Access Web Pages

Most Web pages are written in HTML (Hypertext Markup Language), which can be used by Web browsers on any operating system, such as Windows, Macintosh, and UNIX.

Static Web Pages

Access allows you to export reports, forms, and tables in HTML format. Once you export these database objects, you can publish them as Web pages. These are called static pages because once formed they stand alone from the original database and cannot change when it changes.

To do this, open a table, query, form, or report in your database, use the **File**, **Export** menu command, click the **Save in** drop-down arrow, select a location for the file and enter a **File name** for the Web page. Click the **Save as type** drop-down arrow, and select HTML Documents from the list of save options. Click **Save All**. Enter the name of the HTML template to use for this Web page (if they exist these are usually stored in the '\Program Files\Microsoft Office\Templates\Access' folder) and click **OK**.

A new Web page should have been produced. On it, tables, queries, and forms will all appear as HTML tables, but a report appears in HTML format with the same layout it had in Access.

Active Server Pages

If your Web site accesses your database, and needs to show current data, you can use dynamic pages. Access 2002 provides two ways of exporting reports, forms, and tables in a dynamic Web page format. The more established method is with Active Server Pages, ASP for short. When an .asp file is requested by a Web browser it attempts to retrieve the most current data from its source database. This data is then formatted depending on the layout embedded in the ASP page.

Typical examples common on the Internet are sites that provide continuously updated share price information. They have a central database on their server and the information you receive in your browser is provided on ASP pages, with the file suffix .asp.

Requirements for ASP

To create an ASP file with Access 2002, you need to know the name of the current database, the user name and password to connect to the database, and the URL of the Web server that will store the ASP file. This server must be running Microsoft Active Server 3.0 or later, have the ActiveX Server component installed, along with the Microsoft Access Desktop Driver, and must have access privileges to the database. In other words, this cannot be done lightly and it needs the full co-operation of the Web site administration.

Exporting to an ASP File

In the Database window, click the database object you want to export, action the **File**, **Export** menu command. Click the **Save as type** drop-down arrow, and select Microsoft Active

Server Pages. Click the **Save in** drop-down arrow, and then select the location where you want to save the file. Click **Save**. Enter the name of the HTML template (if one exists), and the name of the database file that contains the data you want the Web server to access. Enter the user name you want the Web server to use to connect to the database and the password you want the Web server to use to log on to the database. Finally enter the Web server URL and click **OK**.

Data Access Pages

Data access pages are written in dynamic HTML or DHTML, which allow dynamic objects in a Web page. They are designed to be viewed by a Web browser but are bound directly to the data in the database. They are shown in an object group in the Database window and can be used like normal Access forms but are, in fact, stored as external files. You can also format data access pages, using many of the same tools you use when creating Access forms.

As long as you have Internet Explorer 5.0 or later installed on your system, you can create a data access page within Access 2002 in Design view, or using a wizard.

Using the Page Wizard

In the Database window, click Pages on the Objects bar, and double-click the **Create data access page by using wizard** option. Select the table and fields that you want to appear in the data access page and click **Next** to continue. Select any fields you want to act as group levels in the Web page and click **Next** to continue. Select the fields to sort the records in the page by, and click **Next** to continue. Enter a title for the data access page and indicate whether you want to **Open the page** in Access or to modify its design in Design view, then click the **Finish** button.

You can also create a data access page with the **File**, **Export** menu command, by selecting Microsoft Access Data Access Page as the **Save as type**.

Alternatively, you can create a data access page by clicking the **New** button on the Database window toolbar, clicking **Design View**, and choosing the table or query you want placed in the data access page.

Viewing a Data Access Page

You can open a data access page from within the database itself or from your Web browser. In the Database window, click **Pages** on the Objects bar and double-click the data access page you want to view. The page opens in a separate window.

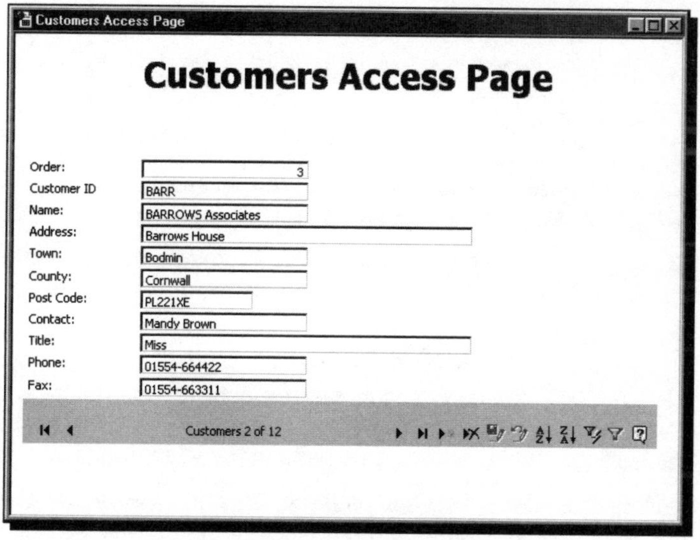

Fig. 11.5 An Access Data Page

We created a data access page from the Customers table of the **Adept 1** database, as shown in Fig. 11.5 above.

The **File, Web Page Preview** menu command will start your Web browser and load a selected data access page, whose data you can then view and edit as you like.

Data access pages contain a navigation bar, as shown in Fig. 11.6 below, to help you retrieve records, filter and sort the data, or search for specific values.

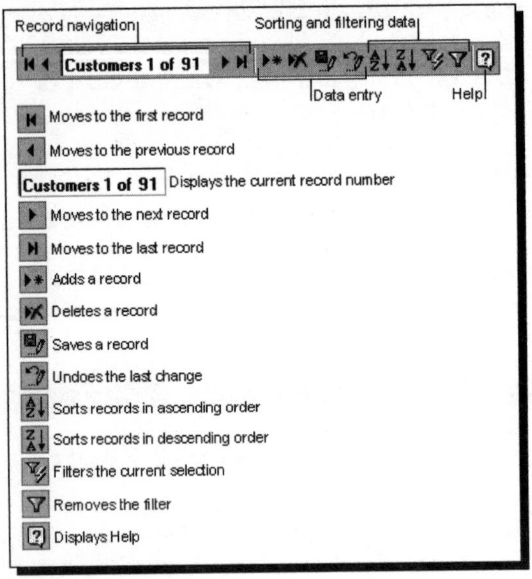

Fig. 11.6 The Data Access Page Navigation Bar

Clicking the Help button opens the Microsoft Access Data Pages Help system if you need more detailed assistance.

Adding a Theme to a Page

Access 2002 has a collection of Web page themes that give you a variety of standard page designs. These control the background, fonts, and colours used in the Web page.

With the data access page in Design view, use the **Format**, **Theme** menu command, select the theme you want to apply and select the theme options you want.

****

Well that's it. We hope you have enjoyed reading this as much as we have enjoyed writing it. A glossary is included next, for reference, and in case you have trouble with any jargon that may have crept in.

12

Glossary of Terms

Access key	A key pressed while holding down the Alt key that allows the user to open a menu, carry out a command, select an object, or move to an object. For example, <Alt+F> opens the File menu.
Action query	A query that copies or changes data.
Active document	An ActiveX document or a document that contains ActiveX controls, Java Applets, or VBScript.
Active window	In an application, the window that appears in the foreground with a highlighted title bar or border to distinguish it from other visible windows.
ActiveX	Microsoft's brand name for the technologies that enable interoperability using the Component Object Model (COM).
ActiveX control	An object that you place on a form to enable or enhance a user's interaction with an application. ActiveX controls have events and can be incorporated into other controls.
Address	A unique number or name that identifies a specific computer or user on a network.
Anonymous FTP	Anonymous FTP allows you to connect to a remote computer and transfer public files back to your local computer

	without the need to have a user ID and password.
ANSI Character Set	American National Standards Institute (ANSI) 8-bit character set used to represent up to 256 characters (0 – 255) using your keyboard.
API	Application programming interface. The set of commands that an application uses to request and carry out lower-level services performed by a computer's operating system.
Applet	A program that can be downloaded over a network and launched on the user's computer.
Application	Software (program) designed to carry out certain activity, such as word processing, or data management.
Archie	Archie is an Internet service that allows you to locate files that can be downloaded via FTP.
Argument	A constant, variable, or expression that supplies additional information to an action, procedure, or method.
Array	A set of sequentially indexed elements having the same intrinsic data type. Each element of an array has a unique identifying index number.
ASCII character set	American Standard Code for Information Interchange (ASCII) 7-bit character set widely used to represent letters and symbols found on a standard U.S. keyboard.
Association	An identification of a filename extension to a program. This lets Windows open the program when its files are selected.

ASP	Active Server Page. File format used for dynamic Web pages that get their data from a server based database.
Assignment statement	A statement that assigns a value to a variable or property. A Set statement assigns an object reference.
Authoring	The process of creating web documents or software.
Automation	A technology that enables applications to provide objects in a consistent way to other applications, development tools, and macro languages.
AVI	Audio Video Interleaved. A Windows multimedia file format for sound and moving pictures.
Backbone	The main transmission lines of the Internet, running at over 45Mbps.
Backup	To make a back-up copy of a file or a disc for safekeeping.
Bandwidth	The range of transmission frequencies a network can use. The greater the bandwidth the more information that can be transferred over a network.
Banner	An advertising graphic shown on a Web page.
BASIC	Beginner's All-purpose Symbolic Instruction Code - a high-level programming language.
BBS	Bulletin Board System, a computer equipped with software and telecoms links that allow it to act as an information host for remote computer systems.

Benchmark	A type of test used to measure hardware and software performance.
Beta test	A test of software that is still under development, by people actually using the software.
Binary format	Machine-readable form. This format is different from ASCII or ANSI formats, which encode data as text.
BinHex	A file conversion format that converts binary files to ASCII text files.
Bit	A binary digit; the smallest unit of data a computer can store. Bits are expressed as 1 or 0.
Bitmap	An image represented by pixels and stored as a collection of bits in which each bit corresponds to one pixel. On colour systems, more than one bit corresponds to each pixel. A bitmap usually has a .bmp file name extension.
Bookmark	For the Internet, a saved reference (in the form of a URL or hyperlink) to a particular location, page, or site, making it easy to return there.
Boolean data type	A data type with only two possible values, True (–1) or False (0). Boolean variables are stored as 16-bit (2-byte) numbers.
Boolean expression	An expression that evaluates to either True or False.
Bound control	A control on a database form, report or data access page that is tied to a field in an underlying table or query.
Browse	A button in some Windows dialogue boxes that lets you view a list of files

	and folders before you make a selection.
Browser	Software that interprets HTML, formats it into Web pages, and displays it to the user. Modern browsers can also contain ActiveX components and can play sound or video files.
Buffer	A temporary holding area in memory where information can be stored.
Bug	An error in coding or logic that causes a program to malfunction.
Button	A graphic element in a dialogue box or toolbar that performs a specified function.
Cache	A special memory subsystem in which frequently used data values are duplicated for quick access.
Card	A removable printed-circuit board that is plugged into a computer expansion slot.
Cascade	The process of one action triggering another action.
Case-sensitive	Capable of distinguishing between uppercase and lowercase letters.
CD-ROM	Compact Disc - Read Only Memory; an optical disc which information may be read from but not written to.
CGI	Common Gateway Interface - a convention for servers to communicate with local applications and allow users to provide information to scripts attached to web pages, usually through forms.

Chart	A graphical view of data that is used to visually display trends, patterns, and comparisons.
Click	To press and release a mouse button once without moving the mouse.
Client application	A Windows application that can accept linked, or embedded, objects.
Client computer	A computer that accesses shared network resources provided by another server computer.
Clipboard	A temporary storage area of memory, where text and graphics are stored with the Windows cut and copy actions.
COM	Component Object Model. An industry-standard architecture for object-oriented development. It defines interfaces on which ActiveX components are built.
Command line	The path, file name, and argument information provided by the user to run a program.
Compaction	A process that gathers or packs memory or storage into as small a space as possible.
Comparison operator	A character, or symbol, indicating a relationship between two or more values or expressions.
Compile error	An error that occurs during compile time as the result of incorrectly constructed code.
Configuration	A general purpose term referring to the way you have your computer set up.
Constant	A named item that retains a constant value throughout the execution of a program.

Context menu	A floating menu that is displayed over a form by right-clicking the mouse. Also called a shortcut, or pop-up, menu.
Control	An object you can place on a form report, or data access page that has its own set of recognised properties, methods, and events.
Control array	A group of controls that share a common name, type, and event procedures.
Cookies	Files stored on your hard drive by your Web browser that hold information for it to use.
CPU	The Central Processing Unit; the main chip that executes all instructions entered into a computer.
Custom control	Now called an ActiveX control.
Data access page	A Web page, created by Access, that has a connection to a database; you can view, add, edit, and manipulate the data in this page.
Data source	The data the user wants to access and its associated operating system, DBMS, and network platform (if any).
Data type	The characteristics of a variable that determine what kind of data the variable can hold.
Database	A set of data related to a particular topic or purpose. A database contains tables and can also contain queries and table relationships, as well as validation criteria.
DBMS	(DataBase Management System). The software used to organise, analyse, and

	modify information stored in a database such as Microsoft Access.
DDE	(Dynamic Data Exchange). A form of communications that uses shared memory to exchange data between applications.
DDL	(Data Definition Language). The language used to describe, change, or define the attributes of a database, especially the layout of tables, columns, and their storage strategy.
Declaration	Non executable code that names a constant, variable, or procedure, and specifies its characteristics, such as its data type.
Default	The command, device or option automatically chosen.
Desktop	The Windows screen working background, on which you place icons, folders, etc.
Device driver	A special file that must be loaded into memory for Windows to be able to address a specific procedure or hardware device.
Dialogue box	A special window displayed by the system, or application, to obtain a response from or provide information to the user.
Dial-up Connection	A popular form of Net connection for the home user, over standard telephone lines.
Directory	An area on disc where information relating to a group of files is kept. Also known as a folder.

Disc	A device on which you can store programs and data.
DLL	(Dynamic-Link Library). A set of routines that can be called from procedures and are loaded and linked into your application at run time.
Docked window	A window that is attached to the frame of the main window.
Document	Any self-contained work created with an application and given a unique file name.
Domain	A group of devices, servers and computers on a network.
Domain Name	The name of an Internet site, for example www.michaelstrang.com, which allows you to reference Internet sites without knowing their true numerical address.
DOS	Disc Operating System. A collection of small specialised programs that allow interaction between user and computer.
Double-click	To quickly press and release a mouse button twice.
DPI	Dots Per Inch - a resolution standard for laser printers.
Drag-and-drop	A combination of features that allow the user to drag an object and drop it onto a form or other object using the mouse.
Dynamic array	An array whose size can change at run time.
Dynaset	A type of Recordset object that returns a dynamic set of pointers to live database data.

EISA	Extended Industry Standard Architecture, for construction of PCs with the Intel 32-bit micro-processor.
E-mail	Electronic Mail - A system that allows computer users to send and receive messages electronically.
Embedded object	An object whose data is stored along with that of its container but that runs in the process space of its server.
Event	An action recognised by an object, such as clicking the mouse or pressing a key, and for which you can write code to respond.
Executable file	A Windows-based application that can run outside the development environment. An executable file has an .exe file name extension.
Expression	Any combination of operators, constants, literal values, functions, and names of fields, controls, and properties that evaluates to a single value.
FAQ	Frequently Asked Questions - A common feature on the Internet, FAQs are files of answers to commonly asked questions.
FAT	The File Allocation Table. An area on disc where information is kept on which part of the disc a file is located.
Field	A category of information stored in a table in a database.
File extension	The suffix following the period in a filename. Windows uses this to identify the source application program. For example .mdb indicates an Access file.

Filename	The name given to a file. In Windows 95 and above this can be up to 256 characters long.
Filter	A set of criteria applied to rows in order to create a subset of the rows.
Firewall	Security measures designed to protect a networked system from unauthorised access.
Flag	A variable used to keep track of a condition in an application. You can set a flag using a constant or combination of constants.
Floppy disc	A removable disc on which information can be stored magnetically.
Focus	The ability to receive mouse clicks or keyboard input at any one time.
Folder	An area used to store a group of files, usually with a common link.
Font	A graphic design representing a set of characters, numbers and symbols.
Form	A window or dialogue box and a container for controls.
FTP	(File Transfer Protocol). A protocol for the transfer of files from one location to another over the Internet.
Function key	Any of the keys labelled F1 to F12. They often provide shortcuts for frequently carried out commands and actions.
GIF	Graphics Interchange Format file. A graphics compressed bitmap format file developed for transmitting images over the Internet.

Graphic	A picture or illustration, also called an image. Formats include GIF, JPG, BMP, PCX, and TIFF.
Graphics card	A device that controls the display on the monitor and other allied functions.
GUI	A Graphic User Interface, such as Windows Me, the software front-end meant to provide an attractive and easy to use interface.
Hard copy	Output on paper.
Hard disc	A device built into the computer for holding programs and data.
Hardware	The equipment that makes up a computer system, excluding the programs or software.
Help	A Windows system that gives you instructions and additional information on using a program.
HTML	Hypertext Markup Language. The main language in which Web documents are written.
HTTP	Hypertext Transfer Protocol. The Internet protocol that delivers information over the Web.
Hyperlink	A location on a page from which a user can go to another page or location. Includes visible text or a graphic and the URL of the destination.
Hypermedia	Hypertext extended to include linked multimedia.
Hypertext	A system that allows documents to be cross-linked so that the reader can explore related links, or documents, by clicking on a highlighted symbol.

Icon	A graphical representation of an object or concept, as a bitmap with a maximum size of 32 x 32 pixels.
Image	See graphic.
Insertion point	A flashing bar that shows where typed text will be entered into a document.
Interface	A device that allows you to connect a computer to its peripherals.
Internet	A worldwide network of thousands of smaller computer networks and millions of personal, commercial, educational, and government, computers.
Intranet	A network within an organisation that uses Internet technologies.
IP	Internet Protocol. The network layer for the TCP/IP protocol suite.
IP address	A 32-bit network address that uniquely identifies a system or device on an intranet or the Internet.
ISA	Industry Standard Architecture; a standard for internal connections in PCs.
ISDN	(Integrated Services Digital Network). A telecom standard using digital transmission technology to support voice, video and data communications applications over regular telephone lines.
ISP	Internet Service Provider - A company that offers access to the Internet.
Java	An object-oriented programming language created by Sun Microsystems for developing applications and applets that are capable of running on any

	computer, regardless of the operating system.
JPG	Joint Photographic Experts Group (JPEG) file. A graphics file format supported by most browsers that was developed for compressing and storing photographic images.
Kilobyte	(KB); 1024 bytes of information or storage space.
LAN	Local Area Network - High-speed, privately-owned network covering a limited geographical area, such as an office or a building.
Laptop	A portable computer small enough to sit on your lap.
LCD	Liquid Crystal Display.
Linked object	An object that is created in one application and linked to another Windows application.
Links	The hypertext connections between Web pages.
Locked	The condition of a data page, row, Recordset object, or Database object, that makes it read-only to all users except the one currently entering data.
Log on	To gain access to a network.
Logic error	A programming error that can cause code to produce incorrect results or stop execution.
MDI	Multiple-Document Interface application, with an MDI form as the container for any MDI child forms in the application.
Megabyte	(MB); 1024 kilobytes of information or storage space.

Megahertz	(MHz); Speed of processor in millions of cycles per second.
Memory	Part of computer consisting of storage elements organised into addressable locations that can hold data and instructions.
Menu	A list of available options in an application.
Menu bar	The horizontal bar that lists the names of menus.
Message	A packet of information passed from one application to another.
Method	A procedure that acts on an object.
MIDI	(Musical Instrument Digital Interface) - enables devices to transmit and receive sound and music messages.
MIME	(Multipurpose Internet Mail Extensions). A messaging standard that allows Internet users to exchange e-mail messages enhanced with graphics, video and voice.
MIPS	(Million Instructions Per Second). Measures the speed of a system.
Modem	Short for Modulator-demodulator devices. An electronic device that lets computers communicate electronically.
Monitor	The display device connected to your PC, also called a screen.
Mouse	A device used to manipulate a pointer around your display and activate processes by pressing buttons.
MPEG	(Motion Picture Experts Group). A video file format offering excellent quality in a relatively small file.

MS-DOS	Microsoft's implementation of the Disc Operating System for PCs.
Multimedia	The use of photographs, music and sound and movie images in a presentation.
Multi-tasking	Performing more than one operation at the same time.
Network	Two or more computers connected together to share resources.
Network server	Central computer which stores files for several linked computers.
Node	Any single computer connected to a network.
Object library	A dynamic-link library (DLL) with one or more type library resources that typically has the extension .olb. You can use the Object Browser to view its contents.
Object module	A module that contains code specific to an object.
ODBC	(Open Database Connectivity). A standard protocol that permits applications to connect to a variety of external database servers or files.
OLE	(Object Linking and Embedding). A special case of ActiveX that enables applications to be created that contain components from various other applications.
Online	Having access to the Internet.
On-line Service	Services such as America On-line and CompuServe that provide content to subscribers and usually connections to the Internet.
Operating system	Software that runs a computer.

Page	An HTML document, or Web site.
Parse	To identify the parts of a statement or expression and then validate those parts against the appropriate programming language rules.
Password	A unique character string used to gain access to a form, network, program, or mailbox.
Path	The location of a file in the folder, or directory, tree.
Peripheral	Any device attached to a PC.
Perl	A popular language for programming CGI applications.
PIF file	Program information file - gives information to Windows about an MS-DOS application.
Pixel	Short for 'picture element'; a dot that represents the smallest graphic unit of measurement on a screen.
Plug-and-play	Hardware which can be plugged into a PC and that can be used immediately without configuration.
Point	In typography, a point is 1/72 of an inch. The size of a font is usually expressed in points.
POP	(Post Office Protocol). A method of storing and returning e-mail.
Pop-up menu	See context menu.
Program	A set of instructions which cause a computer to perform tasks.
Properties window	A window used to display or change properties of a selected form or control at design time.

Property	A named attribute of an object.
Protocol	A set of rules or standards that define how computers communicate with each other.
Query	An instruction to a database to either return a set of records or perform a specified action on a set of records.
RAM	Random Access Memory. The computer's volatile memory. Data held in it is lost when power is switched off.
Read-only	A type of access to data where information can be retrieved but not modified.
Record	A set of related data about a person, place, event, or some other item. Table data is stored in records (rows) in a database.
Recursion	When a procedure calls itself. Uncontrolled recursion usually results in an 'Out of stack space' error message.
Registry	In Windows 95 and higher, the Windows registry serves as a central configuration database for user, application, and computer-specific information.
Relational	A type of database that stores information in tables.
ROM	Read Only Memory. A PC's non-volatile memory. Data is written into this memory at manufacture and is not affected by power loss.
Run time	The time when an application is running.

Scroll bar	A bar that appears at the right side or bottom edge of a window.
SDI	(Single Document Interface). An application that can support only one document at a time.
Search engine	A program that helps users find information across the Internet.
Serial interface	An interface that transfers data as individual bits.
Server	The system designed to share data with client applications; servers and clients are often connected over a network.
Shortcut key	A function key or key combination, such as F5 or <Ctrl+A>, that executes a command.
Shortcut menu	See context menu.
Site	A place on the Internet. Every Web page has a location where it resides which is called its site.
SLIP	(Serial Line Internet Protocol). A method of Internet connection that enables computers to use phone lines and a modem to connect to the Internet without having to connect to a host.
Socket	An endpoint for sending and receiving data between computers.
Software	The programs and instructions that control your PC, like Access and Office.
SQL	(Structured Query Language). A language used in querying, updating, and managing relational databases.

Stack	A fixed amount of memory used to preserve local variables and arguments during procedure calls.
Standard control	An intrinsic control included in the Office Toolbox.
Surfing	The process of looking around the Internet.
SVGA	Super Video Graphics Array; it has all the VGA modes but with 256, or more, colours.
Syntax	The prescribed order and punctuation for putting programming language elements into statements that are meaningful to the programming language.
System disc	A disc containing files to enable a PC to start up.
Tab order	The order in which the focus moves from one field to the next as the Tab or <Shift+Tab> keys are pressed.
Table	The basic unit of data storage in a relational database. A table stores data in records (rows) and fields (columns).
TCP/IP	(Transmission Control Protocol/Internet Protocol). The Internet standard for transferring data among networked computers.
Text file	An unformatted file of text characters saved in ASCII format.
TIFF	Tag Image File Format - a popular graphic image file format.
Toggle	To turn an action on and off with the same switch.

Toolbar	A bar containing icons giving quick access to commands.
Twip	A screen-independent unit used to ensure that placement and proportion of screen elements in your screen application are the same on all display systems. A twip is a unit of screen measurement equal to 1/20 of a printer's point.
UNIX	Multitasking, multi-user computer operating system that is run by many computers that are connected to the Internet.
Upload/Download	The process of transferring files between computers. Files are uploaded from your computer to another and downloaded from another computer to your own.
URL	(Uniform Resource Locator). An address to an object, document, or page or other destination on the Internet or an intranet.
VBScript	(Visual Basic Script). Microsoft's Internet scripting technology, based on Visual Basic
Virus	A malicious program, downloaded from a web site or disc, designed to wipe out information on your computer.
WAIS	(Wide Area Information Server). A Net-wide system for looking up specific information in Internet databases.
WAV	Waveform Audio (.wav) - a common audio file format for DOS/Windows computers.

Web	A network of hypertext-based multimedia information servers. Browsers are used to view any information on the Web.
Web Page	An HTML document that is accessible on the Web.
Wildcard characters	The asterisk (*), question mark (?), hash sign (#), exclamation mark (!), hyphen (-), and brackets ([ ]) can all be wildcard characters. They can be used in queries and expressions to include all records, file names, or other items that begin with specific characters or match a certain pattern.
Windows API	The Windows Application Programming Interface consists of the functions, messages, data structures, data types, and statements you can use in creating applications that run under Microsoft Windows.
WinSock	Windows Sockets is a standard way for Windows-based programs to work with TCP/IP.
Wizard	A Microsoft tool that asks you questions and then creates an object depending on your answers.
World Wide Web	A system for navigating the Internet by using hyperlinks. With a browser, such as Internet Explorer, the Web appears as a collection of documents, controls, pictures, sounds, and digital movies.

Index

Companion Discs

COMPANION DISCS are available for many of the computer books written by the same author(s) and published by BERNARD BABANI (publishing) LTD, as listed at the front of this book (except for those marked with an asterisk). These books contain many pages of file/program listings. There is no reason why you should spend hours typing them into your computer, unless you wish to do so, or need the practice.

ORDERING INSTRUCTIONS

To obtain companion discs, fill in the order form below, or a copy of it, enclose a cheque (payable to **P.R.M. Oliver**) or a postal order, and send it to the address given below. **Make sure you fill in your name and address** and specify the book number and title in your order.

Book No.	Book Name	Unit Price	Total Price
BP		£3.50	
BP		£3.50	
BP		£3.50	
Name		Sub-total	£............
Address		P & P (@ 45p/disc)	£............
		Total Due	£............
Send to: P.R.M. Oliver, West Trevarth House, West Trevarth Nr Redruth, Cornwall TR16 5TJ			

PLEASE NOTE

The author(s) are fully responsible for providing this Companion Disc service. The publishers of this book accept no responsibility for the supply, quality, or magnetic contents of the disc, or in respect of any damage, or injury that might be suffered or caused by its use.